William Ewart Gladstone

Plant-Life

Popular papers on the phenomena of botany. With 148 illustrations drawn by the

author and engraved by W.M.R. Quick

William Ewart Gladstone

Plant-Life
Popular papers on the phenomena of botany. With 148 illustrations drawn by the author and engraved by W.M.R. Quick

ISBN/EAN: 9783337095253

Printed in Europe, USA, Canada, Australia, Japan

Cover: Foto ©Andreas Hilbeck / pixelio.de

More available books at **www.hansebooks.com**

Popular Papers on the Phenomena of Botany

WITH *148 ILLUSTRATIONS DRAWN BY THE AUTHOR*

AND ENGRAVED BY W. M. R. QUICK

LONDON

MARSHALL JAPP & COMPANY

MDCCCLXXXI

TO THE

OFFICERS AND MEMBERS

OF

THE LAMBETH FIELD CLUB

THESE PAPERS ARE

𝔇𝔢𝔡𝔦𝔠𝔞𝔱𝔢𝔡

BY THEIR

FELLOW-MEMBER AND PAST-PRESIDENT

THE AUTHOR.

"It certainly is a marked advantage in the study of natural history that it leads you on by the hand; it inveigles you, if I may say so, into learning what is good and what is useful. Many a one might have his mind first opened to the attractions of natural history, which mind, if once opened, might perhaps be capable of applying itself beneficially to harder and more repulsive studies. These analogies of natural history are invaluable; they have a most gracious effect in developing the finer faculties of the mind; they establish a connection between the different portions of creation."—Right Hon. W. E. GLADSTONE, M.P.

CONTENTS.

—o—

CHAPTER I.

CONTENTS.

CHAPTER X.

CHAPTER XI.

CHAPTER XII.

CHAPTER XIII.

CHAPTER XIV.

LIST OF ILLUSTRATIONS.

——o——

NOTE.—Figs. 93, 95, 96, 97, 98, 99, 100, are from " Ferns and Ferneries."

PLANT-LIFE.

—o—

CHAPTER I.

MICROSCOPIC PLANTS.

NOT the least among the discoveries which we owe
to the microscope is the existence of an extensive,
though exceedingly minute, world of animal and
plant life. No matter where we look, we shall find
members of this hitherto invisible world absolutely
swarming around us. The very air we breathe is
filled with minute forms of life; and in the water we
drink we are certain to find many of them, unless it
has been boiled or filtered. Any sweet fluid which
has been exposed to the air for a few hours will teem
with them; so will water in which any vegetable or
animal matter has been infused. Some are so exceedingly small that 20,000 of them placed side by
side would not cover the length of an inch. Very
expensive and finely-adjusted instruments are, of
course, required to enable us to see organisms so
extremely minute; but there are hundreds of interesting forms which may be clearly seen by simpler
and less expensive instruments. One of the best

A

means of obtaining these low forms of vegetation is to collect a quantity of Duckweed, "the green mantle of the standing pool," from the surface of a stagnant pond, together with some of the water. If a single plant of Duckweed be put on a glass slip and covered with the thin glass used for the purpose, then placed under the microscope, a number of distinct forms will be seen—some vegetable, some animal. With the latter we have nothing to do in the present volume ; we shall simply ignore them.

Most of the minute plants found in ponds belong to the same tribe as the Seaweeds (the *Algæ*), but we shall also have something to say of the tiny representatives of the Mushroom family (the *Fungi*), low forms of which abound on all decaying substances.

One of the simplest of the Algæ—and one of the most plentiful—is the *Protococcus.* Our readers will probably be struck with the fact that these very small plants have very large names. We hope they will not be frightened, for, after all, it is a small matter; and when they are learnt, they give us some fact about the owner, such as it would take many words in English to make clear. In this instance it means literally *first berry or plant*, that is, the simplest form of plant. It is found in abundance in ponds, ditches, rain-water butts, and in fact wherever water accumulates in little pools. It consists of a single cell or sac containing a jelly-like substance called *protoplasm.* It is this protoplasm which constitutes the living part of the plant; the covering (cell) cannot grow, it requires to be added to by the protoplasm secreting fresh deposits of it. Some of the specimens, you will notice, are coloured green, some red, and others parti-coloured. This is owing to certain portions or granules of the protoplasm being covered with a peculiar pigment called *chlorophyll* (leaf-colour), which is either green or red. The cell-wall itself, though seemingly coloured, is colourless. If we examine a number of these with our microscopes we shall probably be able to observe the manner in which the plant is increased, for it does not produce seeds like flowering plants. The alternative plan adopted by the gardener to increase his stock of plants is to take cuttings from them, and we find that a somewhat similar process goes on in this Protococcus, for it divides itself into two parts, and then again into four. This cut will show you how it is done. A partition forms across the protoplasm, and thus two cells are formed inside the old cell-wall; these two cells divide in the same manner, and the old cell-wall bursts, setting free four perfect *proto-cocci*. Sometimes, though rarely,

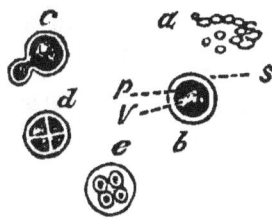

Fig. 1.

a little protuberance or swelling is formed at one part of the plant, and, gradually increasing in size, assumes a round form, and ultimately becomes separated from the parent cell. At times a remarkable change takes place in this plant. The protoplasm penetrates the cell-wall at two points, and protrudes in the form of two long, slender filaments (*cilia*), which, being kept constantly moving, propel the cell rapidly along. Like many other of these minute forms of life, Protococci are not easily destroyed. Shallow pools containing them may be thoroughly dried up by a very hot summer, yet as soon as rain falls the Protococci may be found there in profusion. When in a dry state they are often carried long distances by the wind, and, catching on any damp surface, quickly increase in numbers. Consequently, one has but to look in damp places to find a profusion of them. If we care to experiment a little with this one-celled plant, we may find out much that will be useful to us in the study of Physiological Botany. If, for instance, we place some Protococci in rain-water, and watch them from day to day, we shall observe that they thrive well, and multiply rapidly. This proves that the Protococcus can build up its cell-wall and protoplasm out of the substances contained in the rain-water. Now the only substances found in fresh rain-water are *carbonic anhydride*, *ammonium nitrate*, and a few mineral salts which were suspended in the air as dust; and a chemist would tell us that the protoplasm consists of a substance called *protein*, fat, and mineral salts, whilst the cell-wall is composed of *cellulose* and a few of the mineral salts. This chemist may be a very clever man, but if you ask him to make some protein, fat, or cellulose out of the carbonic anhydride, ammonium nitrate, &c., he will honestly acknowledge his inability to do so, because protein, fat, and cellulose are *organic* compounds, and only to be found in animal or vegetable substances. From this we are forced to the conclusion that some remarkable changes must go on in this tiny cell to enable it to build up its protoplasm and cell-wall out of such seemingly unpromising material; and perhaps in the course of our microscopical researches we may come across some plants which will throw a little more light upon this subject; but for the present we must bid adieu to Protococcus, and see what else we have under our microscope.

A long narrow rod, with transparent walls ornamented with spiral bands of green. It is one of the Yoke-threads or *Con-fervæ*, those minute hair-like plants you have so often seen

Fig. 2.

in ponds. You observe it is made up of a number of joints; these are cells, each like a protococcus with its sides flattened. The spiral ornament is really the protoplasm so arranged round the interior of the cell-wall. Each cell is capable of sustaining life, and giving rise to a new plant. They increase in length by the cells dividing across their width; they increase in numbers by the protoplasm becoming broken up into many little oval bodies, each provided with two *cilia* or hair-like appendages, by the constant lashing of which they propel themselves through the water. When the protoplasm becomes thus broken up, the cell-wall opens and sets them free, each one ultimately becoming a separate plant. It is called the *Zygnæma*, a term which signifies yoke-thread.

By gently moving our glass slide we become aware of the presence of another of the same tribe of plants

—*Confervæ*—one of the *Oscillatoriæ.* It is very similar in appearance to Zygnæma, but is much narrower,

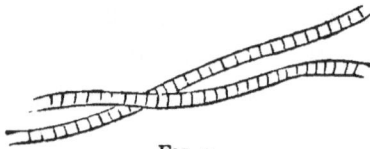

FIG. 3.

and the cells are very short. Now look at them under the microscope; they are gently moving over each other in all directions. It is from this peculiarity—this *oscillating* motion—they derive their name. Mr. Berkeley says of this tribe of plants :—

"*Oscillatoriæ* grow in various situations—in salt and fresh water, on damp ground, amongst grass on close-shaved lawns, like lichens on the trunks of trees, floating on the surface of lakes and seas, or suspended like a cloud, giving rise to variously coloured waters. One or two fine purple species form thick woolly fleeces in the hotter parts of India, while many inhabit hot springs."

You think it strange that these low forms of plant life should have the power of motion, but that is only because you have been in the habit of observing large trees and bushes which are fixed to the ground by strong branched roots. Yet even these have certain powers of movement—at any rate, during portions of their lives. Have you not observed how plants bend towards the light, and how some that in the morning inclined to the east, in the evening lean to the west? Then look at climbing plants, how they move round a stick or string. Mr. Darwin, the great naturalist, has written a book devoted entirely to the "Movements and Habits of Climbing Plants," and probably we shall come across a few instances of movement in the higher plants in the present volume.

Whilst we have been talking another specimen has come into the field of vision; and if you are not quick, you will lose a sight of it. It is the *Pandorina morum*, and it consists of a round cell containing a large number of smaller round cells or spores, each spore provided with two cilia, which protrude through the wall of the larger containing cell.

Fig. 4.

But I have here, on another slide, a more remarkable and most beautiful form of similar construction. This is the *Volvox globator*, a species that once puzzled scientific men considerably, to assign the department of nature to which it belonged. Some considered it was an animalcule, others thought it was a plant, but it has now been satisfactorily settled that it is a plant. It is a most beautiful object under our microscope, as it moves majestically across the field of vision, revolving continually by means of the multitude of cilia with which its surface is studded. These cilia are disposed in pairs, as will be seen on reference to the illustration, and each pair marks the presence of a cell. These cells are united by very fine threads, and within the sphere thus formed the young *Volvoces* revolve.

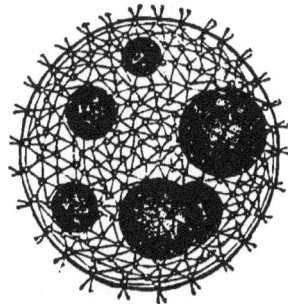

Fig. 5.

Where found, they are usually in great profusion—in fact, the water in some ponds is perfectly green, owing to their presence in vast numbers, but you can seldom place reliance upon any particular pond for containing it. It is to be found during all seasons—when the rains of spring have swollen the ponds, when the summer or autumn sun has reduced their circumference, and when they are covered with two or three inches of ice—they may still be found. But you may find *Volvox* in profusion in a pond to-day, whilst in a week, a month, or a year, you may search diligently and long in the same water without the slightest success.

There is another active little plant you are sure to find in a pond—the *Euglena viridis.* It is of a bright green colour, generally tapering towards each extremity, and having a red spot, like an eye, at one end. This is really not an eye, but due to some change in a portion of its chlorophyll. Sometimes specimens will be found possessing a long delicate

FIG. 6.

filament (*flagellum*), as in the illustration, and Mr. M. H. Robson * has recently called attention to the fact that this *flagellum* is sometimes bulbed at its extremity (fig. 6, *c*). What is the use of this bulb has not been yet explained, but it is suggested it may be used as a sucker to enable it to cling to surfaces.

Some of the most beautiful forms will be found among the *Diatoms* and *Desmids.* A few of these will be seen in figs. 7, 8, 9, 10, 11, 12, and 13. Fig. 7 is that of a desmid (*Cosmarium*) in the act of divi-

* See "Science Gossip," 1879, pp. 159, 231.

sion. Fig. 8 is a lovely form called *Closterium*, found
in myriads at the bottom of ponds. In both these

FIG. 7.　　　　FIG. 8.　　　　FIG. 9.　　　　FIG. 10.

species the plant consists of two cells. In fig. 9
(*Pediastrum*) there are a large number of cells united
into a spherical form, each cell having two processes
from it which give the compound plant a stellate
appearance. In *Scenedesmus* (fig. 10) the cells are
united side by side, and the two extreme cells of the
series are provided with long filaments. These all
belong to the order of *Desmids*. They are totally
distinct from the Diatoms—which we shall allude
to presently—but in several points they somewhat
resemble them. Multiplication takes place by division, though in a somewhat peculiar manner. Thus
fig. 7 shows Cosmarium dividing ; the two outer cells
formed the old plant, and the inner ones are those
newly formed. The next change to take place would.
be a division between the two new cells, and thus
two separate plants would be formed, each consisting
of a new and an old cell. The same process goes on
in the other Desmids. The *Diatoms* (figs. 11, 12, 13)
are all encased in little boxes, composed of pure
flint formed into two valves, one of which fits into
the other, just as a pill-box fits into the lid. They
are not green like the Desmids, but yellow-brown.
Like *Volvox*, the *Desmids*, and other plants, the
Diatoms have been claimed as members of the

animal kingdom, but their title to be regarded as
plants has been long since thoroughly established.

FIG. 11.

FIG. 12.   FIG. 13.

They are, of course, exceedingly minute; and it frequently happens that in summer ponds are dried up,
and the Diatoms and other low plants are carried
long distances by the wind. We may then look in
vain among the dry mud of the late pond for active
Diatoms. We shall find what appear to be their
empty valves, the protoplasm having become dried
up by the sun. Yet if these are again placed in
water they will revive almost immediately, and as
soon as the rainy season commences we may search
in the refilled ponds and find Diatoms in their former
abundance.

Long after the plant itself is dead the flint valves
retain their form, and consequently geologists find
vast beds and strata of rocks composed entirely of
them. The earth, called Tripoli, used in polishing,
consists almost entirely of their empty cases. Dr.
Hooker says: "The phonolite stones of the Rhine,
and the Tripoli stones, contain species identical with
what are now contributing to form a sedimentary
deposit, and, perhaps, at some future period a bed
of rock extending in one continuous stratum for
400 measured miles. I allude to the shores of the
Victoria Barrier, along whose coasts the soundings

examined were invariably charged with diatomaceous remains, constituting a bank which stretches 200 miles north from the base of the Victoria Barrier, while the average depth of water above it is 300 fathoms, or 1800 feet. Vast quantities, again, occur in beds under the guise of a white powder, which is called mountain meal, and is actually mixed with flour in some parts of Sweden, though it is perfectly inert, and can serve merely to increase the bulk of the food."

Mr. W. H. Shrubsole, F.G.S., has recently discovered the presence of these ubiquitous organisms in the London Clay formation. About twenty species have already been identified, but there are also a number of species new to micro-scopists. Mr. Shrubsole reports that he has traced the diatomaceous zone for several miles, and is still pursuing the inquiry.

FIG. 14.

Some of the water-snails and other molluscs subsist largely upon these Diatoms, and many rare species have been obtained from the stomachs of fish. They can endure the greatest degree of cold without injury to their vital powers, and some have been found in hot springs.

All these plants we have mentioned belong to the group of *Algæ;* they all possess *chlorophyll*, and are able to live upon the most simple chemical compounds. We have next to glance at a group of plants which never possess this chlorophyll, and can only live on organised matter. To commence with, we could not have a better subject than the Yeast-plant (*Torula*), which plays such an important part in the manufacture of beer.

Each Yeast-plant consists, like Protococcus, of a single cell containing protoplasm, which has a clear space (*vacuole*) in it. The cell-wall consists of a substance called *cellulose*, of which all wood is composed; it has no vitality, and therefore cannot grow, but is increased by fresh deposits formed by the *protoplasm*. On being chemically analysed, it is found to consist of carbon, hydrogen, oxygen, nitrogen, sulphur, and small quantities of other elements, which are arranged in the form of protein, fat, and cellulose, much the same as in protococcus. In the latter plant we saw that it had the power of building up these substances out of such simple compounds as *carbonic anhydride, ammonium nitrate*, and a few mineral salts, all of which are found in rain-water. But if we place *Torula* in rain-water, it cannot grow at all. To enable it to grow, we must place it in a fluid containing sugar, ammonium tartrate, and mineral salts. If we place this solution, with a little

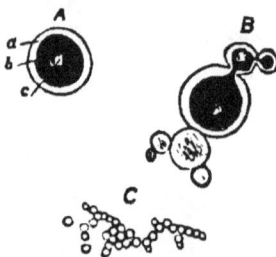

Fig. 15.

yeast, in a bottle, and keep it corked up for a day or two, the cork will probably be driven out with great force and a mighty effervescence will take place in the fluid. If we now fix a glass tube through the cork, and securely fasten an empty bladder to the upper end, we shall see that it will gradually become filled with gas. If we are chemists,

we can easily find out what gas it is. We test it, and
find it to be carbonic acid gas. How is this? There
was no carbonic acid gas in the fluid. We analyse
the fluid again, and find that the sugar has disappeared. And so we proceed with our experiments;
and, in the end, see clearly that the oxygen has been
taken out of the sugar by the Torula, and the carbonic acid gas set free; in fact, it has been feeding
upon the sugar. Now Protococcus is able to get its
food from the carbonic acid gas, and sets free *oxygen*.
Torula *can't* obtain its oxygen from carbonic acid
gas, or it would have multiplied in the rain-water.
There is evidently some remarkable difference in
these plants. Protococcus possesses *chlorophyll*, by
means of which it is able—under the influence of
sunlight—to decompose carbonic acid gas. Torula
does *not* possess chlorophyll, and therefore has to get
its food from a substance already formed by plants.
This it finds in the sugar, which contains both carbon
and oxygen. Torula exists as well in the dark as
in the light; Protococcus cannot exist in the dark.
If we apply a small quantity of iodine to both, we
find that Torula remains unchanged, while Protococcus turns *blue*. This denotes that it contains
starch, a substance peculiar to green plants; on the
other hand, Torula agrees with the *Fungi* in possessing neither starch nor chlorophyll, and in being
independent of light. Protococcus we may take as
a simple type of the green plants, and Torula of the
Fungi.

If we take a tiny drop of the yeast on the head
of a pin, touch a glass slide with it, and, carefully

putting on a cover-glass, examine it with a high power, we shall see a multitude of these little plants arranged in strings and heaps. Each plant ranges in size from $\frac{1}{2500}$th to $\frac{1}{7000}$th part of an inch across, or an average of about $\frac{1}{3000}$th. In other words, it would take 3000 of these plants, placed side by side, to cover the length of an inch. They increase in numbers by budding. A slight protuberance arises at one part of the cell-wall, and, rapidly growing, assumes the same form and size as the cell from which it sprung; though, perhaps, before it gets so large, it has itself produced a bud, which has in turn produced another. So they multiply at an enormous rate, and their growth causes the fermentation of fluids containing sugar, which, by the subtraction of some of its elements, is changed into alcohol, the intoxicating element in beer, wines, and spirits. These Torulæ are capable of being dried into a powder, and in such a condition they form an article of commerce, for their vitality is not impaired. They may be kept in this state for a considerable period, but on introducing a very small quantity into a sugary liquid, fermentation will ensue almost immediately as the result of their renewed activity and growth. We have ourselves kept yeast for nearly three years without injury to it.

But it is time we advanced a step in the consideration of these minute fungi. We have here a specimen of green mould, such as grows on all decaying substances—old bread, old boots, jam, dead leaves, &c. Carefully selecting a small portion, we place it under a low power, and find something like our illustration.

Its name is of the same alarming proportions as those
we have previously experienced ; it is the *Penicillium
glaucum.* It consists of a number
of cells, like Torula, drawn out
into an oblong form, and placed
end to end. Each of these cells
has the same structure as Torula,
consisting of a cell-wall, and protoplasmic contents. As these cells
grow, cell-walls are formed trans-
versely, and thus the number of
cells increased. The string of cells
so formed is termed a *hypha.* They
run along horizontally, sending

FIG. 16.

off at intervals branches, some of which penetrate
downwards into the substance on which the plant is
growing, and some rise upwards into the air. The
descending branches are termed the *submerged hyphæ*,
the ascending *aerial hyphæ*, whilst those which run
along the surface form a network, and are known as
the *mycelium.* The submerged hyphæ serve as roots
to nourish the plant, and the aerial hyphæ, when
they have reached a certain height, produce at their
summits a chain of *round cells* very like Torulæ.
These are the *spores.* They serve the same purpose as
—though they must not be confounded with—seeds,
that is, to produce other plants like that on which
they were formed. When a spore falls upon a suitable surface, the cell-wall is pushed out at one or
more points, and each protuberance lengthens into a
long tube or hypha, divided at certain distances by
cross partitions. From this ascending and descend-

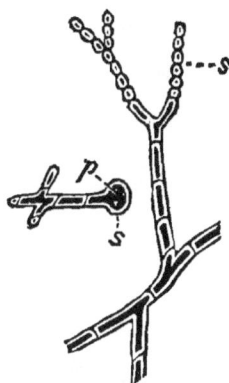

ing branches are given off, and we soon have a complete colony of moulds.

Another mould (*Mucor mucedo*) bears a considerable resemblance to the last, though the plant is not divided into a number of cells, but is one continuous cell. A large round cell is formed at the summit of an aerial hypha, the protoplasm of which divides into a number of smaller cells. These are the *spores*, and the large cell in which they are formed is called the *sporangia*. The wall of the *sporangia* bursts and scatters the spores.

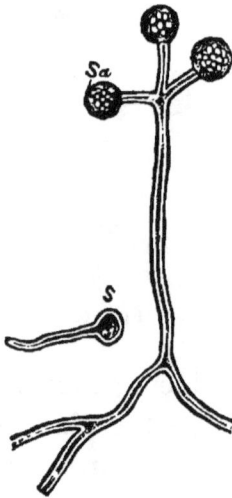

An interesting thing about many of these fungi is what is termed *polymorphism*, or many forms. Thus Torula is believed by some scientific men to be merely a form of some mould like Penicillium or Mucor, and that the difference in form depends upon the substance they are growing on or in. Penicillium has been found to give rise, under certain conditions, to another form previously ranked as an independent species of *Eurotium*. In *Puccinia graminis* (fig. 18) and *Æcidium berbcridis* (fig. 19) there is a remarkable interchange of form, according to the plant on which it is parasitical. *Puccinia* is the "rust" which farmers find so destructive to wheat, whilst *Æcidium* is a parasite upon the Berberry. There is an old agricultural belief that Berberry bushes near cornfields

FIG. 17.

are the cause of mildewed corn, and recent scientific
investigations have shown that there is truth in the

Fig. 18.   Fig. 19.

belief, which is not always the case with popular
adages. Dr. M. C. Cooke, in his "Fungi," gives the
following :—

"There is a village in Norfolk, not far from Great
Yarmouth, called 'Mildew Rollesby,' because of its
unenviable notoriety in days past for mildewed corn,
produced, it was said, by the Berberry bushes, which
were cut down, and then mildew disappeared from
the cornfields, so that Rollesby no longer merited its
sobriquet. It has already been shown that the corn-
mildew (*Puccinia graminis*) is dimorphous, having a
one-celled fruit (*Trichobasis*), as well as a two-celled
fruit (*Puccinia*). The fungus which attacks the Berberry is a species of Cluster-cup (*Æcidium berberidis*)
in which little cup-like peridia, containing bright
orange pseudospores, are produced in tufts or clusters
on the green leaves, together with their spermogonia.
De Bary's observations on this association of forms
were published in 1865. In view of the popular
belief, he determined to sow the spores of *Puccinia
graminis* on the leaves of the Berberry. For this
purpose he selected the septate resting spores from
Poa pratensis and *Triticum repens*. Having caused
the spores to germinate in a moist atmosphere, he

B

placed fragments of the leaves on which they had
developed their secondary spores on young, but full-
grown, Berberry leaves, under the same atmospheric
conditions. In from twenty-four to forty-eight hours
a quantity of the germinating threads had bored
through the walls and penetrated amongst the sub-
jacent cells. This took place both on the upper and
under surface of the leaves. Since, in former experiments, it appeared that the spores would penetrate
only in those cases where the plant was adapted to
develop the parasite, the connection between *P.
graminis* and *Æcid. berberidis* seemed more than
ever probable. In about ten days the spermogonia
appeared. After a time the cut leaves began to
decay, so that the fungus never got beyond the
spermogonial stage. · Some three-year-old seedlings
were then taken, and the germinating resting spores
applied as before. The plants were kept under a
bell glass from twenty-four to forty-eight hours, and
then exposed to the air, like other plants. From the
sixth to the tenth day, yellow spots appeared, with
single spermogonia; from the ninth to the twelfth,
spermogonia appeared in numbers on either surface;
and a few days later, on the under surface of the
leaves, the cylindrical sporangia of the *Æcidium* made
their appearance, exactly as in the normally developed parasites, except that they were longer from
being protected from external agents. . . . It seems,
then, indubitable so far that *Æcidium berberidis* does
spring from the spores of *Puccinia graminis*."

Other experiments have been made in which the
spores of *Æcidium* have been placed on healthy

plants of rye, and in five or six days after, these plants were affected with rust, whilst the remainder of the crop was unaffected.   Dr. Cooke, in his valuable book, gives detailed instances of other species in which this polymorphism occurs.

Fig. 20 is a representation of a small portion of the Potato fungus (*Peronospora infestans*), which at times destroys the entire crop in large districts.   It is produced by spores which, falling on the Potato plant, develop, and their hyphæ enter the stomata or breathing-pores of the leaf, and penetrating its cellular tissue, absorb all nutriment from it. From the leaf the hyphæ or mycelium traverse the substance of the stem, and finally reach the cells of the tuber — the Potato

FIG. 20.

itself.   Mr. Worthington G. Smith has recently made some valuable researches into the life-history of this fungus, with the result of adding considerably to our knowledge of it.   Fig. 21 is a modified reproduction, on a small scale, of one of that gentleman's illustrations, representing the section of a small portion of potato leaf.   *a, a* are two of the hairs with which the leaf is furnished; *b, b,* and *c, c,* the cellular tissue of the leaf.   *d* is a branch of the fungus emerging from a breathing-pore or stomate, and "is no other than a continuation of a thread of spawn or mycelium which lives inside, and at the expense of the assimilated material of the leaf. When this thread emerges into the air, as here shown, it speedily ramifies in different directions, and bears fruit at the tips of the branches, as at *e, e;* these fruits are termed simple spores, or conidia, because from their smallness they are dust - like. It is quite possible they may be an early state of the vesicles which contain the zoospores, as seen at *f, g.* However this may be, they

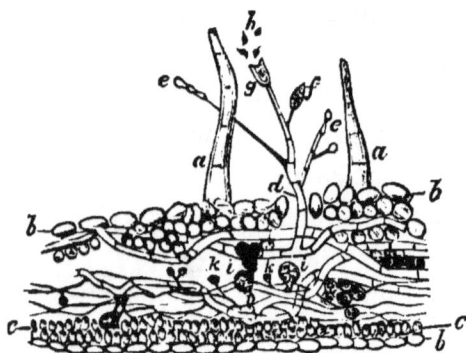

Fig. 21.

are commonly arrested in growth while still small, and they germinate in an exactly similar manner with the zoospores themselves, and may be considered somewhat analogous with seeds. The Potato fungus has another method of reproducing itself in the 'swarm spores,' as shown at *f, g.* These are so called because, on the application of moisture (as supplied by rain or dew, or when applied artificially), the vesicles set free a swarm of from six to fifteen or sixteen other bodies known as 'zoospores,' so named because they are furnished with two lash-like tails, and are capable of moving rapidly about like animalcules. This rapid movement usually lasts for about half an hour, and (like the dust-like conidia, or 'simple spores,' before mentioned) the swarm spores generally enter the breathing-pores of the leaf, and there germinate. So potent, however, are the contents of these bodies when set free, that they are capable of at once corroding, boring, and entering the epidermis of the leaf, or even the stem or tuber itself. These zoospores are best seen when within the vesicle f, where they arise from a differentiation of the contents; but when once set free (h), they are, from the extreme rapidity of their movements, very difficult to make out. In almost half an hour they cease to move, their lash-like tails (cilia) disappear, and having burst at one end, a transparent tube is protruded, which is a similar mycelium in every respect with that produced by the simple spore, and which grows, branches, and fruits in a precisely similar manner." *

But besides these zoospores and simple spores, the Potato fungus produces a third kind called "oospores," which were unknown until Mr. Smith's careful study of the fungus by night and day through its various changes and developments revealed its existence. Referring to our fig. 21 again, we notice several large, round cells marked i, and some smaller k. The larger is the oogonium, and the smaller the antheridium. The oogonium is analogous to the ovary, and the antheridium to the anther, in flowering plants. These two bodies come in contact, and the antheridium pushes out a small tube which enters the cell-wall of the oogonium, and through it a portion of the antheridium contents is emptied into the oogonium. This fertilises the oospores which are contained within, and when the latter are mature the mycelium vanishes, and the resting spores are set free. It sinks into the earth, and remains quiet during the winter,

* Worthington G. Smith, "Monthly Microscopical Journal," 1875.

but on the return of spring it germinates, and if potatoes are not near perishes.   But if it is within reach of a potato tuber, it enters it; its mycelium penetrates the haulm, and coming out into the air develops zoospores and conidia, and thus repeats the life-history given by Mr. Smith.   From the experiments made with it, it is clear that a wet season is the most favourable to its growth, and the potato has less chance of recovering from its attack; but it is to be hoped that with the information recently obtained with reference to it, scientific men may be soon in a position to give such advice as will enable agriculturists to cope with this potent enemy.

Fig. 22 represents another of these fungi which, like the Potato fungus, largely affect cultivators of the soil.   This is the *Oidium Tuckeri*, or Vine Blight, which attacks the Continental vineyards and even the hothouse vines in our own country; frequently it is

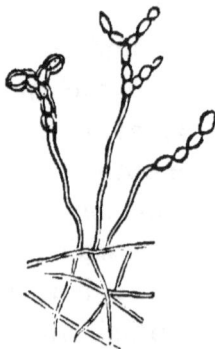

FIG. 22.

FIG. 23.

the cause of great destruction.   Recently it has been ascertained to be only one form of the fungus shown at fig. 23—*Erysiphe*, a species of which attacks the pea.   There is besides a very large number of these small moulds which attack various species of plants and fruits.   A species of *Peronospora* (*P. effusa*) attacks spinach; another (*P. gangliformis*) is very injurious to lettuces ; *P. Schleideniana* destroys young onions, and *P. trifoliorum* attacks the lucerne.

Exigencies of space compel us to close this chapter, though the number and variety of microscopic plants entitle them to a whole volume; but perhaps sufficient has been said to show the reader that a large amount of recreation and instruction may be obtained by a study of these low forms of plant-life.

CHAPTER II.

PLANT STRUCTURE AND GROWTH.

ALL plants commence existence as a single cell, like *Torula* or *Protococcus*, and it is only by the multiplication of these cells, the alteration of their form by pressure against each other, and their development into tubes, &c., that we get the wonderfully varied and beautiful forms of higher plant life. As we have seen, the lowest forms of plants are *unicellular*, but from these to the complex organisation of the forest trees there is a very gradual advance. In the same group as *Protococcus*—the *Algæ*—we have plants with a larger number of cells, as *Zygnæma* and *Oscillatoria*. In the division of *Fungi* we have a similar advance from the simple form of *Torula*, through the moulds with strings of cells placed end to end, up to the mushrooms and toadstools. From the remarks in the previous chapter, it will be seen that plants are divided into two great groups, those that possess *chlorophyll*—green plants—and those that do not—fungi.

The green plants are again broken up into other divisions, according to the complexity of their organisation.

In *Zygnæma* we have seen how the normal form

of the cell is modified by contact at their ends, changing them from the oval or round form of *Protococcus* into an oblong. In higher plants, we may find them of every conceivable shape, but the modification is always due to this same cause—pressure; but we shall find it is exerted at the sides as well as at the ends.

Here in this diagram, at *a*, we have two cells scarcely touching at their sides, so that they retain

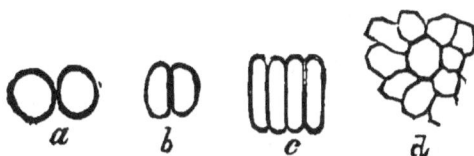

FIG. 24.

their simple form; but at *b* we suppose them to be pressed together, and this pressure alters their form, making flat the two sides that are pressed together. At *c* we suppose that a number of cells are placed side by side, and pressure exerted at both ends of the series, consequently they assume an oblong shape. At *d* they are pressed together from all sides, just as people are pressed together in a crowd, and the result is, the cells become many-sided (*polyhedral*), so as to occupy the least amount of space. Now in different parts of a plant we have these cells arranged and modified in different ways, and groups of cells arranged in a definite manner are termed *tissues*. The simplest form is *cellular* tissue, the cells composing it retaining much of the normal form, but frequently they become many-sided by the pres-

sure of neighbouring cells.   It comprises several varieties, of which the most important is *Parenchyma*,

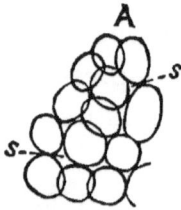

FIG. 25.   FIG. 26.

in which the cells are so
arranged as to leave spa-
ces (*intercellular spaces*),
through which air can cir-
culate between the cells.
It forms the principal portion of most plants, the
other tissues being embedded in it.

Another form of cellular tissue is called *Sclerenchyma*, from the cells being hard, owing to the thickening of the cell-wall.   The "stones" of cherries,
plums, &c., are composed of sclerenchyma.

Some of the cells assume a long, narrow, drawn-out
form, like fibres or tubes, and from their appearing in
compact masses among the *parenchyma*, they are

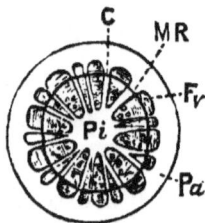

FIG. 27.   FIG. 28.

known as *fibro - vascular
bundles*.   It is these bundles
which form the midrib and
"veins" of leaves and the
hard part of the stem.
They are made up of *wood-
tissue, bast-tissue,* and *vascular tissue,* packed together
in wedge - shaped masses

(fig. 27).   On examining a cross section of one of
these wedges with the microscope, we find it presents the appearance of fig. 28.   *o* is the outer, *i* the
inner end ; B is the bast-tissue, C the *cambium zone,*
W wood-cells, and V the openings of the spiral
vessels and ducts.

The *bast-tissue* consists of very long, thin cells, drawn out like threads, and very tough. The *wood-tissue* is likewise composed of long cells, which fit into each other closely, but the cells are not nearly so long as those of the bast. The bast-tissue supplies the *bast* of the gardener, hemp, flax, and Russia-matting.

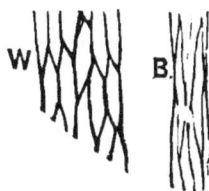

FIG. 29.
W. wood-tissue.
B. bast-tissue.

The *cambium zone* is a narrow band of small, thin-walled cells, which retain their power of growth and division. It lies between the bast and the wood, and is continually producing *bast-tissue* on the outer side, and *wood-tissue* on the inner.

Some cells which are united by their ends absorb the cell-walls which separate them from the cell immediately above or below them, and thus form a long, open tube. Cells which have been thus modified are called *ducts* and *vessels*.

In these a process of thickening the cell-wall goes on, but instead of the new *cellulose* being deposited equally over the whole inner surface of the cell, cer-

FIG. 30. FIG. 31. FIG. 32. FIG. 33.

tain portions are left unthickened, and the result is to make them appear *dotted* or *pitted;* these are known as dotted cells or vessels (fig. 30); in others it is deposited in the form of a *spiral* thread, and these are called *spiral vessels* (fig. 31). Another method in which the thickening takes place is in the form of rings, and such cells are known as *annular vessels* (fig. 32). In others, again, which are four or five sided, the new deposits take place in the form of thin bars across the sides, and as they thus bear a resemblance to the "rounds" of a ladder, they are termed *scalariform vessels* (fig. 33).

All these tissues have a definite place in the structure (excepting the lowest forms) of plants. No matter how they may be arranged *inside* a plant, the outside of it is always invested by a layer of flat, close-fitting, colourless cells, called the *Epidermis.* Dotted over this epidermis are a number of little holes, each surrounded by two kidney-shaped cells (fig. 34). These orifices are termed *Stomates*, or mouths, because they are used for breathing purposes. Each stomate communicates with the intercellular spaces we spoke about just now, and through them carbonic acid gas is absorbed from the atmosphere.

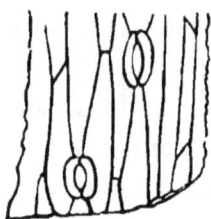

FIG. 34.

This is the internal structure of a plant; with its external characters, we suspect, most of our readers are tolerably familiar, yet for those who are not, we will give a brief account of it.

Fig. 35 represents the ideal plant. We observe that it consists of a main stem, more or less branched at its two ends. The branches at the upper portion of the stem bear *leaves* and *flowers*,—those at the lower end of the stem bear neither, and are called roots. These latter serve a double purpose,—they fix the plant in the earth, and also imbibe moisture from it. *They are never green*, and they avoid the light. The stem, on the contrary, is ever seeking the light, and usually green. The leaf is a thin, flat plate attached by a stalk to the stem or branch. Fig. 36 represents a thin slice cut through the thickness of a leaf. Ep shows the colourless epidermic cells bounding the upper and lower surfaces of the leaf. Beneath them is the green-celled parenchyma, and between these layers of parenchyma, which are closely packed, there are others loosely arranged (LP) to form the intercellular spaces (IS).

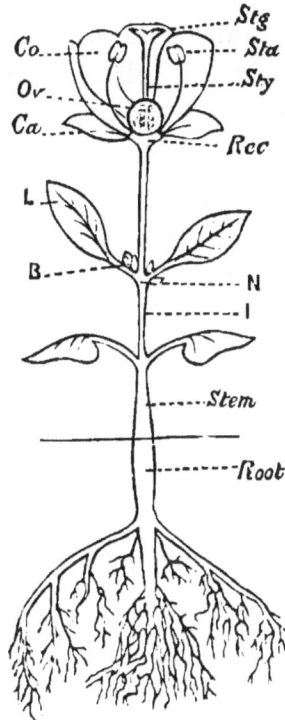

FIG. 35.

Within this are seen the fibro-vascular bundles (Fv). St marks the presence of the stomates.

The food of a plant is of two kinds—liquid and gaseous. The liquid food is obtained from the soil through the roots, and consists of water in which various mineral salts are dissolved. These salts con-

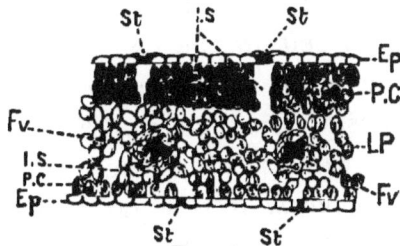

FIG. 36.

tain iron, nitrogen, potash, phosphorus, and sulphur; they abound in most soils, but cannot be
taken up by the plant in a solid form, hence, if a
plant be kept without water, it cannot obtain any
mineral salts. The gaseous food is obtained from
the atmosphere through the stomates of the leaf. It
consists of carbonic acid gas, which is composed of
carbon and oxygen. The chlorophyll-bearing cells
have the power of retaining the carbon and setting
the oxygen free; but it can only do so when under
the influence of sunshine. On entering the stomates,
the gas circulates through the intercellular spaces to
the chlorophyll cells, and through the spiral vessels
to the fibro-vascular bundles.

As the roots absorb the liquid food (*sap*) from the
ground, it passes from cell to cell, and through certain vessels of the fibro-vascular bundle until it
reaches the leaves. The warmth of the sun causes
the water in the leaf-cells to evaporate—that is, to fly
off through the intercellular spaces and the stomates
in the form of a light vapour. If a plant exposed to
the sun be not well supplied with water at the roots,
it will quickly fade and die, in consequence of this
great evaporation robbing the cells of their moisture.
As the water evaporates, it is perfectly pure, all the
mineral substances it previously contained having
been left in the cells. The carbon absorbed from
the air is combined with the cell-sap, and forms a
substance called *starch.* Of this starch *cellulose* for
the cell-walls is formed, and it is also changed by the
protoplasm into sugar and fat. By the addition of
nitrogen and sulphur (taken · up in water by the

roots) to the constituent parts of starch, protoplasm has the power of forming *albuminoids*, of which protoplasm itself is formed, and dependent upon for growth and increase.

This process of manufacturing various substances out of these simple materials is termed *assimilation.* The substances formed by assimilation are stored up in the cells for future use in nourishing the plant. Thus in the potato, which is a part of the stem, the protoplasm of the cells is thickly dotted with grains of starch, it being laid up in the tuber to provide nourishment for the new shoots (eyes). In the wheat, oat, rice, pea, and bean we find it stored up in the seeds for the nourishment of the young plant or embryo, whilst it is developing its roots and leaves. The presence of starch in a plant may always be detected by the application of a slight quantity of iodine to the cell, when, if it contains starch, it will be stained blue. Oils and fats are also stored up as food for the plant in the same manner as starch; they are specially abundant in such plants as the Flax (from the seeds of which linseed-oil is obtained), Cocoa-nut, Olive, and the Castor-oil plant. Sugar, unlike starch, exists in a *liquid* state, and abounds chiefly in the stem of the sugar-cane and the tap-roots of parsnip and beet. It is manufactured by the plant from starch. A variety of substances, also formed in the cells, are known under the general term of *alkaloids*. Many of them have exceedingly valuable properties, and form important objects of commerce. Some of them are used in medicine, as morphia from the opium poppy, aconite from monkshood, quinine from the bark of the *chinchona*, and strychnine from the seeds of *Nux vomica.* Tea and coffee owe their well-known refreshing qualities to the presence of certain alkaloids in their cells.

The *albuminoids* are stored up in the protoplasm of active, living cells, and in many seeds in the form of *albumen*, &c. Other substances in small quantities are also stored up in the cells, as sulphur, iron, potash, silica, lime, phosphorus, magnesia, &c.

The conditions necessary for the growth of plants are soil, air, moisture, and heat above the freezing-point. The quantity or degree required varies with the species, some requiring great depths of soil in which to develop their roots, others requiring but little, whilst in the case of misletoe and some tropical species of orchids soil is quite unnecessary, the plants growing on the trunks of trees. Some water-plants have the whole surfaces of their leaves and stems submerged, and therefore must be dependent on the water for their carbon. Many ferns and bog-plants require copious supplies of moisture, whilst succulent plants, as the Stonecrops and Houseleeks, delight in dry, stony places. With respect to heat, plants are widely distributed over the whole surface of the globe. The colder regions produce very few species, and those sparingly, but in hot, damp countries vegetation is very profuse.

CHAPTER III.

THE FERTILISATION OF FLOWERS.

It is popularly held that the chief end of plants is to minister to man's sense of the beautiful in form and colour, but the recent investigations of scientific men should dissipate so presumptuous a theory. Man certainly does—unless his nature be very depraved—derive very great pleasure from the presence of flowers; but *the* purpose of the fine odours, the varied tints and exquisite forms of flowers is that the species shall be continued by the production of healthy seeds. How they are instrumental in effecting this we will explain.

A flower usually consists of four series of organs, differing widely in form and office, but all modifications of the simple leaf. These are the *calyx*, consisting of leaves called *sepals ;* the *corolla* formed of leaves called

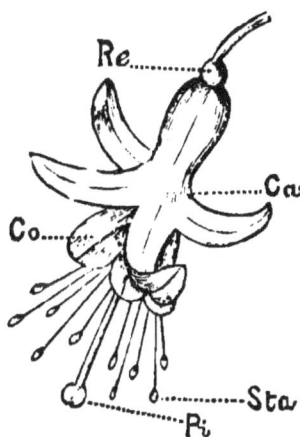

Fig. 37.

petals ; the *stamens*, and the *pistil*. The calyx and the corolla are known as the *floral envelopes;* the

c

stamens and pistil are the *essential organs*, because

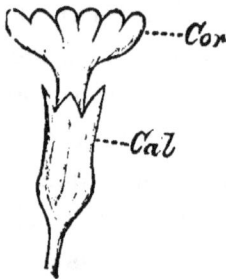

FIG. 38.

they are necessary for the production of seeds. The calyx is
usually green; the corolla generally conspicuous from its bright
colours. In some plants the
calyx or the corolla is entirely
wanting, in which case the floral
covering is termed a *perianth*, as
in the Crocus and Lily.

The stamens consist of two parts, the *filament* or
stalk (F), and the *anther* or pollen-case (An). The an-

FIG. 39.

ther is the principal part of the organ, and
is filled with a very fine powder like flour.
When the anther is ripe, it splits open,
and sets free this powder, or *pollen* as it is
called. Examined under the microscope,
this pollen is seen to consist of very
minute cells filled with protoplasm (fig.
40). The *pistil* occupies the centre of the
flower, and is surrounded by the stamens
when these are present. It consists of
three parts—the *stigma* or surface, the
style or stalk, and the *ovary* at its base.

The ovary contains the immature seeds or ovules,
which require to be fertilised by the contents of a
pollen grain before they can grow into perfect seeds.
The style may be absent, and the stigma placed
directly on the ovary. The stigma is either sticky,
rough, or covered with long hairs, to retain the pollen
grains. In some plants the stamens are found in one
flower and the pistil in another; they are then termed

unisexual. If both are found in the same flower, it
is *bisexual.* Sometimes, again, the staminate flowers

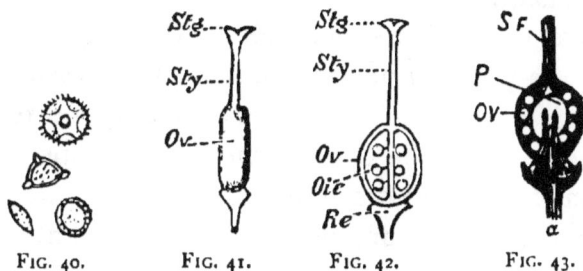

FIG. 40.   FIG. 41.   FIG. 42.   FIG. 43.

are produced on one plant, the pistillate on another.
In this case they are known as *diœcious* plants. If
both are found on the same plant, they are *mon-
œcious.* To effect fertilisation, some of this pollen
must be conveyed from the anther to the stigma.
Supposing a pollen grain adheres to the stigma,
the moisture of that organ induces it to send
out from its under side a very slender
shoot, the pollen tube, which pierces
the stigma and, increasing in length,
penetrates the whole length of the style,
finally entering the ovary, where it
comes in contact with an ovule. As the
result of this contact, the protoplasm of

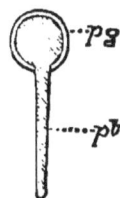

FIG. 44.

the pollen tube mingles with that of the ovule, cell
division takes place, and the seed gradually ripens.

But before this can take place, certain difficulties
must be overcome. If the pollen-bearing (staminate)
flowers are on one plant, and the pistillate flowers on
another, how is the pollen to be placed on the stigma?
Again, in those flowers which possess both stamens
and pistil, the stamens open and discharge their

pollen in such a way that it cannot possibly fall on the stigma. In the Fuchsia flower of fig. 37, nothing seems easier, from the inverted position of the flower, than that the pollen should fall on the stigma; but in reality the position of this renders such a result more difficult, for the sticky surface can only be reached from below. In the Crocus the anthers open along their backs so as to discharge their pollen away from the stigma. There are many other remarkable contrivances in various plants actually to prevent the pollen being shed on the stigma.

The lesson of this is: it is not to the plant's benefit, but otherwise, that its own pollen should fertilise its seeds; and on experimenting with various plants, to ascertain the truth of this, it is found that all plants fertilised with pollen from another individual produce far more robust offspring than the plant which is fertilised 'by its own pollen. Indeed, in some plants the application of its own pollen to its stigma has had the effect of causing the pistil to shrivel up, and the flower to die. Why this *is* so we cannot tell; but it is beyond doubt a fact, applicable to the animal as well as the vegetable kingdom, that the offspring of individuals closely related are more or less sickly and weak. Seeing that Nature objects, as a rule, to *self*-fertilisation, we should naturally expect to find that she has taken means to ensure their *cross*-fertilisation.

The untiring observations of Darwin, Lubbock, and Müller have clearly shown that such contrivances are as plentiful as they are remarkable—in fact, some of them are absolutely startling in the delicacy and efficiency of their mechanism. First, it is necessary that carrying agents should be employed to convey the pollen; and we find that of these there are two classes—the *wind* and various *insects*. These are Flora's carriers, whom she intrusts with a most delicate mission, and that they perform it well we may see by the lavish manner in which the fields, the lanes, and woods are adorned with living gems.

Flowers which are fertilised by the wind are *never* conspicuously coloured; and here we find the reason why flowers are brightly coloured. If we observe an organ in any plant or animal which is of no apparent use to it, we may be sure that it has had a use in the past, among the ancestors of the species, for Nature does not provide organs or adornments unnecessarily. However beautiful in appearance may be a flower, we shall find on closer acquaintance that its beauty is not merely to gratify our sense of the beautiful, but to serve a useful purpose in the economy of Nature, and with special reference to the species possessing it. Thus there is not a single wind-fertilised * flower that is highly coloured, because its colouring would be unnecessary; on the contrary, nearly all insect-fertilised † flowers are brightly and conspicuously coloured. Taken in conjunction with other facts which we shall adduce, the reason for this is sufficiently obvious—the bright hues are to attract insects to the flower. Again, wind-fertilised flowers produce vast quantities of pollen; insect-fertilised flowers produce very little. In the first case, the pollen being carried, as in the fir, from tree to tree,

* *Anemophilous.*   † *Entomophilous.*

great quantities must be lost in transit by being blown in a direction where there are no other trees of the species, or by falling to the ground. Therefore it is necessary that very large quantities should be produced to ensure that the small amount requisite for fertilisation should reach its proper destination. But in flowers fertilised by insects no such risk is run, therefore only a small amount of pollen is produced.

Then, too, we find a marked difference in the stigma of a wind-fertilised as compared with an insect-fertilised plant, which will be best explained by reference to these diagrams. Fig. 45 shows the stigmas of Wheat and Hop, which are anemophilous; fig. 46 those of the Primrose and Heath, which are entomophilous. In fig. 45 it will be observed the

a   b

FIG. 45.

a   b

FIG. 46.

stigmas are more branched and hairy, the object, of course, being to offer a larger surface to catch the wind-borne pollen grains. In fig. 46, of insect-fertilised plants, the stigmas are of a simpler form. We have remarked that the colours of flowers are for the attraction of insects, and to prove this we must show that insects are sensible to colour. The experiments of Sir John Lubbock, who has added so much to our knowledge of insects, show this conclu-

sively.   He says: " That bees are attracted by, and
can distinguish, colours was no doubt a just inference
from the observations on their relations to flowers;
but I am not cognisant of any direct evidence on the
subject.   I thought it, therefore, worth while to make
some experiments; and a selection from them will
be recorded in the forthcoming volume of 'Journal
of the Linnean Society.'   I placed slips of glass
with honey on paper of various colours, accustoming
different bees to visit special colours, and when they
had made a few visits to honey on paper of a particular colour, I found that if the papers were trans-
posed the bees followed the colours." *

If bees in a garden are watched, they will be seen
to confine their attention to one particular species,
though they have been observed to be incapable of
distinguishing between certain closely-related species,
though this may indicate that they are not true species,
but only varieties.

Most flowers which have an *irregular* corolla—that
is, with the petals unequal in size and form—are,
according to Mr. Darwin, insect-fertilised; and he
says it is very probable that those species which are
habitually self-fertilised receive fresh vigour from an
occasional cross.   Sir John Lubbock, in his charming
book, has entered fully into the question as affecting
our native wild plants, and has given examples from
most of the natural orders and families.   It is impossible in the small space at present at our disposal to
do more than give a few of the most striking illustrations.   Why should the bees and other insects go to

* Wild Flowers in Relation to Insects, p. 12.

all this trouble? What benefit do they derive from the transaction? These are questions which will probably have occurred ere this to the reader's mind. They are easily answered by the facts—so, too, are many others in connection with flowers that used to puzzle people to explain satisfactorily. Why are flowers provided with honey and sweet perfumes? Why are flowers highly coloured? Why do flowers "go to sleep"—*i.e.*, close their petals—at night, and in rainy weather?

These and many other questions are answered by modern science satisfactorily. The insects are attracted from a distance by the perfume of the flower; they are shown the exact spot by the colour of the corolla; and they evidently are aware, from inherited instinct, that sweet odours and bright hues are the outward signs of a store of honey. The insects find their reward in the honey; the honey, then, is only a bait to induce the insect to visit the flower, and detach and carry the pollen. Flowers which are fertilised by bees or butterflies, which fly by day, close their petals at night, for it would not be to their advantage to have their honey stolen by night-flying moths, who cannot fertilise them. On the contrary, night-flowering plants keep the petals closed during the day, because they are fertilised by moths; and to render them conspicuous they are light in colour. Thus, the White Campion, which flowers at night, is of a silver-white hue, and the light-yellow Evening Primrose has the additional assistance of a very strong sweet perfume. Flowers, too, close in rainy weather to protect their honey. Many flowers which

depend upon the honey for their fertilisation are
specially constructed to protect it. The honey is
generally so situated in flowers that to get at it the
insect is bound to push itself against the anthers, and
when it retires it takes away some of the pollen
on its body or head. The stigmas and anthers are
usually so placed that on visiting the next flower the
pollen on the insect comes into contact with the
stigma, and is detached.

In some cases the stamens and stigmas do not
ripen at the same time, so that it is impossible for
the plant to be self-fertilised. This is the case with
the common Arum, in which the stigmas come to
maturity before the anthers. Any one
acquainted with the flowers of this plant
—and few persons are not—will understand that it is impossible for the pollen
to be blown out of the flower after it has
been shed by the anthers; and though,
from their being placed above the stigmas,
it would seem an easy matter for self-
fertilisation to take place, this is prevented
by the stigmas maturing before the pollen
is ripe; so that if it is to be fertilised at

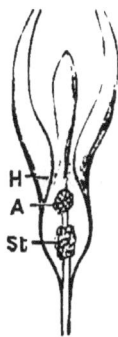

Fig. 47.

all, it must be by pollen being brought from a plant
which has flowered a little earlier, and in which the
stigmas have passed maturity. Just above the band
of anthers (A) are a number of hairs (H) pointing
downwards. Small insects in quest of honey easily
pass these hairs and reach the bottom, but on wish-
ing to return, these same hairs, from their direction,
form an effectual barrier, and the insects remain

prisoners until the stigmas have passed maturity. Each stigma secretes a drop of honey as a sort of payment to the insects. The anthers ripen and discharge their pollen, which falling to the bottom, dusts the insects. The hairs shrivel up and set free the prisoners, who are probably soon shut up in another flower, which they fertilise with the pollen obtained unconsciously from their first prison. This is the only method in which fertilisation could possibly take place in the Arum. Sir John Lubbock states that sometimes more than a hundred small flies will be found in a single Arum.

In many other plants the same result is attained by the anthers maturing before the stigmas, so that an insect which had visited a flower with mature *anthers* coming upon one with mature *stigmas* would be almost certain to deposit some of the pollen obtained from the former. Self-fertilisation in these is out of the question. As an illustration, take the

FIG. 48.   FIG. 49.

Common Pink of our gardens. Fig. 48 shows a flower of this plant soon after expanding its corolla.

The centre of the disc is occupied by five anthers, which shed their pollen and shrivel up. Their place is then taken by five more anthers which have been hitherto concealed in the flower-tube, but when they have shed their pollen and retired, they are succeeded by the stigmas, which are only now ripe. If an insect visit one of the younger flowers it can hardly fail to brush off some of the pollen, which is almost equally certain to be deposited on the stigmas of an older flower. But more remarkable is the case of the Forget-me-Not, in which the young flowers have the stigma protruding a little above the disc, so that an insect which has dusted itself with the pollen from a neighbouring flower is pretty sure to fertilise it. But should this not happen, the plant fertilises itself; the corolla-tube lengthens, so as to bring the stamens up to a level with the stigma, when pollen is sure to get deposited on the stigma.

In the Violets and Pansy there is a most curious arrangement by means of which the pollen is showered down on the bee from above. One of the petals is developed back into a hollow spur, in which the honey is secreted. The anthers are so arranged that they form a box into which the pollen is deposited by the anthers. Through the centre of this chamber the pistil passes, the stigma protruding; it should also be noted that the

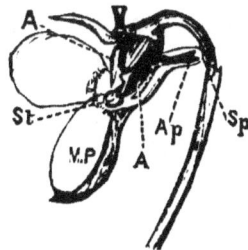

FIG. 50.

pistil is bent in a peculiar manner, and that two of the anthers have long processes which go back into the spur. The bee on visiting the flower, alights on the median petal (MP), and its weight, by depressing the petals, probably forces the side of the spur (Sp) against the anther processes (Ap), the effect of which is to unlock the ring of anthers (A). The bee's head also strikes against the stigma, which causes the loose dry pollen to fall on the bee's face. On visiting another flower this pollen will be deposited on the under-surface of the stigma. It is remarkable that in this species the pollen is dry and loose, whilst in most entomophilous flowers it is sufficiently sticky to adhere to the anthers, but in this case the bee does not rub against the anther, therefore if the pollen were not loose and dry, fertilisation could not take place.

In the pretty little Milkwort (*Polygala vulgaris*) again, we have a different arrangement. The petals form a tube to which the stamens are attached in two bundles near the top. Below these is the stigma, and behind it a viscid disc. The proboscis of an insect pushed down this tube in search of honey comes in contact with the viscid disc, and is thus rendered adhesive. When it is withdrawn it touches against the anthers and carries off some of the pollen to be deposited on another flower.

In the Mallows (*Malva*) we have good evidence of the truth of the theory that the object of colour in flowers is to attract insects. We have two species of Mallows growing in the same locality, *Malva sylvestris* and *M. rotundifolia*. *Sylvestris* is fertilised by insects, *rotundifolia* fertilises itself, and is seldom visited by insects. *Sylvestris* has large conspicuous flowers, *rotundifolia* has small ones. In the former the stamens and stigmas are so arranged that self-fertilisation is impossible; in the latter they are so placed that self-fertilisation cannot be avoided. A similar instance occurs among the species of Willow-herbs (*Epilobium*).

Among the various species of Wild Geranium we have some with large flowers and some with small. Of the large-flowered species we will take *Geranium pratense* as the type. Its flowers are erect and opened wide by day; at night they hang down partially closed. When the flower first opens the pistil is immature. It is divided into five stigmatic lobes, and when immature these lobes have the stigmatic surfaces in contact, as shown in fig. 51*a*. When the flower opens the ten stamens also are immature and lie flat on the petals. Five of them become matured and raise themselves parallel with the pistil, shed their pollen and retire to their former position. They are succeeded by the other five, and when these have retired the stigmas unfold as in fig. 51*b*. From this it will be seen the flower cannot fertilise itself. But in the smaller species, of which the well-known Herb Robert (*G. Robertianum*) is an example, the stigmas are mature before all the pollen is shed, so that if cross-fertilisation does not take place self-fertilisation does. Here the size of the flowers is evidently due to the visits of insects, and no doubt Sir John Lubbock is right when he remarks: "It would seem that, as a

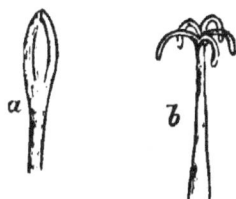

FIG. 51.

general rule, where we find within the limits of one
genus some species which are much more conspicuous than others, we may suspect that they are also
more dependent on the visits of insects."

Among the plants with papilionaceous flowers there
is a remarkable arrangement of the petals and stamens
to ensure cross-fertilisation.   In these flowers—of
which the Pea, Bean, Lupin, Broom, and Laburnum
are examples—the corolla consists of five petals, as
in fig. 52. The upper one (S) is called the "Standard,"

 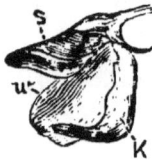  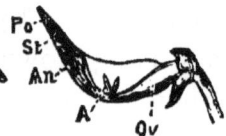

FIG. 52.   FIG. 53.   FIG. 54.   FIG. 55.

the two lateral ones (W) are called "Wings," and the
two lower ones (K) are united at their lower edges,
and form what is known as the "Keel."   Within this
keel the stamens and pistil lie hidden, and the honey-
glands are also contained.   To get at the honey the
insect has to alight on the wings which form a con-
venient platform for the purpose.   Fig. 53 shows a
flower of the Lupin with one of these wings removed.
The wings are so locked to the keel that the weight
of the insect, whilst pressing down the wings, presses
down the keel also.   From the curvature of the
stamens (fig. 55, An) this has the effect of forcing out
some of the pollen which has previously been shed
within the tip of the keel.   Fig. 54 shows the wings
depressed and the pollen being forced out from the
tip of the keel against the bee's body.   When the

pollen is all exhausted the stigma is protruded in the very same place, so that if it should press against a bee which has thus obtained pollen from a younger flower, cross-fertilisation is certain. The mechanism by which this is effected may be easily seen if any papilionaceous flower be taken and gentle pressure exerted on the wings. The tip of the keel will be exposed and a thin curl of pollen forced out, just as it would be against the bee's body.

Every one is familiar with the flowers of *Tropæolum major*, better known as the Nasturtium. The corolla is continued backwards as a long hollow spur which contains the honey. When the flower first opens all the organs are immature, but soon an anther becomes mature and erects itself in front of the entrance to the spur, so that no bee could get at the honey without pushing against the anther. All the other stamens erect themselves in like manner, one at the time, until all the pollen is shed, when they hang down out of the way, and the pistil, which has been slowly maturing and lengthening, raises itself to the position previously occupied by the stamens. Insects which have visited young flowers cannot help fertilising older ones when they visit them. Self-fertilisation cannot take place.

The Primrose, Cowslip, &c., are well known to have two forms of flowers. Even the children are acquainted with this peculiarity of the genus, and call them " thrum-eyed " and " pin-eyed," according as the stigma or stamens are most prominent. In the one form (fig. 56) the pistil is elongated and the stigma on a level with the top of the corolla-tube. In

the other form (fig. 57) the mouth of the corolla-tube
is occupied by the anthers, and the stigma is half way
down the corolla-tube. These forms are termed "long-
styled" and "short-styled." Now it would seem
an easy matter for self-fertilisation to take place in
the "short-styled" flower, for the pollen could easily
fall on the stigma, and probably this does take place;
but Mr. Darwin has shown us that such contact
seldom produces good seed. On the other hand self-
fertilisation is impossible in the "long-styled" form,
for the pollen on being shed falls to the bottom of

FIG. 56.   FIG. 57.

the tube. There is another difference in these two
forms—the short-styled form produces pollen grains
which are *one-third* larger than those of the long-
styled form, so that a pollen-grain from the long-
styled form would not contain sufficient material to
penetrate the whole length of its own style. Such
arrangements as this demonstrate most clearly the
pains Nature has taken to ensure cross-fertilisation.
It will be seen from the cuts that an insect visiting
the long-styled flower, in pushing its proboscis down
to the bottom of the tube, where the honey-glands
are, would dust it with pollen at a part which, when

it visited a short-styled flower, would be likely to touch against the stigma; or if it first visited a short-styled flower, its head would strike against the anthers, and, when visiting a long-styled flower, deposit the pollen so obtained on the stigma.

More remarkable, perhaps, in this respect is the Purple Loosestrife (*Lythrum salicaria*), in which three forms occur. In the first form the pistil is very long and the stigma is far above the anthers, which are in two sets—six of them being about two-thirds of the length of the pistil, and six about one-third. In the second form six stamens are as long as No. 1's pistil, whilst No. 2's pistil is two-thirds of that length, and the other six stamens are one-third. In the third form the pistil corresponds in length with the short stamens in the other forms, whilst one set of stamens are of the length of No. 2's pistil, and the other set agree with the pistil of No. 1. The long stamens produce large pollen grains to fertilise the long pistils; the short stamens produce small pollen, and the middling-size stamens produce pollen of a size half-way between these two extremes.

Most Umbelliferous plants—such as the Carrot, Parsley, Parsnip—have very small flowers, inconspicuous individually, but from the manner in which they are associated in large flat heads, they are among the most noticeable objects of the hedgerows. They are fertilised chiefly by small insects to whom the honey is easily accessible, it being secreted on a flat open disc, and therefore it is inaccessible to Lepidoptera and bees with long trunks. At first only the anthers are mature, but when they have shed their

D

pollen and shrivelled up, the stigmas mature. Self-fertilisation cannot take place. The more conspicuous these flowers are rendered by association, the larger the number of insects by which they are visited.

In Viburnum (Guelder Rose) the flowers are arranged on a similar principle to the *Umbellifers*, but the outer circle of flowers produce neither stamens nor pistil, the corolla being developed to a very large size instead. This has the effect of rendering the flower-head very conspicuous, and, together with the powerful perfume exhaled, is an attraction to the insects, who ramble over the flowers collecting and depositing pollen as they go. For this they are rewarded with a plentiful supply of honey.

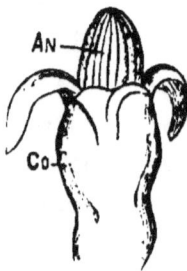 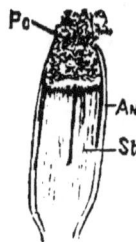 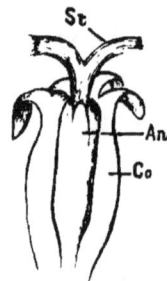

FIG. 58.   FIG. 59.   FIG. 60.

In the Composite order of plants we have a similar arrangement, of which the Common Daisy may be taken as a type. The "flower" of this plant is in reality a cluster of flowers or "florets." The advantages of this arrangement are—(1) the flowers are rendered more conspicuous; (2) the honey is more easily accessible from the close proximity of the flowers, consequently more insects visit it; and (3)

in passing over the flower-head one insect fertilises
several florets.   There are nearly ten thousand known
species of this order, but the structure of the flower
is tolerably uniform, and can be well observed in the
Daisy or Feverfew.   In the latter the stamens are
united so as to form a tube, enclosing the pistil.   The
pistil is furnished at top with a brush of hairs.   The
anthers ripen before the stigmas, and shed the pollen
on their inner surface, so that it is deposited in the
tube on the top of the immature stigmas which it
cannot affect.   The pistil as it ripens elongates and
pushes up the pollen, which is thus brought in the
way of insects.   By means of the brush every pollen
grain is swept out before the stigmas ripen.   When
this has been effected, the stigmas raise themselves
from the tube, and assume a position as in fig. 60.

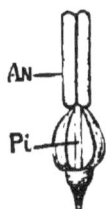 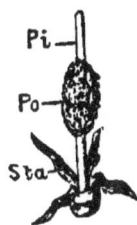 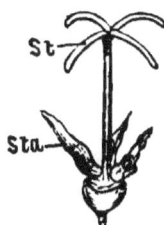

FIG. 61.   FIG. 62.   FIG. 63.

The flowers of the various species of Harebell
(*Campanula*) are more or less inverted, and among
the most graceful objects of our native flora.   At first
both pistil and stamens are immature, the stamens
clasping the pistil (fig. 61).   The anthers ripen, shed
their pollen on the style, and shrivel up.   Insects
visiting the flower clasp the style, and thus remove
the pollen.   The pistil then elongates, and the stigmas

open, as in fig. 63. From the inverted position of
the flower self-fertilisation is as difficult here as in
Fuchsia (p. 36).

Exigencies of space prevent us doing more, under
this head, than calling attention to a very beautiful
and interesting order of plants, to a description of the
fertilisation of which Mr. Darwin has devoted a large

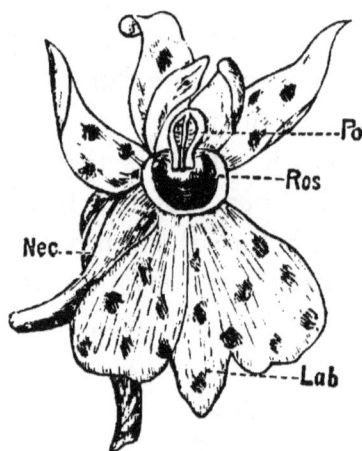

FIG. 64.

volume. We allude to the Orchids, about the strange
forms of which we may have something to say in a
future chapter. Certainly no more remarkable instance of the adaptation of plants to their insect-
fertilisers could be found outside this group of plants.
In the Common Purple Orchis the pollen is produced
in two club-shaped masses, the *pollinia*, as in figs. 64,
65, and 66. The stigma is a viscid disc below the
pollinia. Part of the corolla forms a platform on
which the insects alight (*labellum*), and it is continued
downwards and backwards as a tube (*nectary*), in
which the honey is secreted. To get at the honey

the insect must alight on the labellum, and in pushing its proboscis down the nectary, strikes its head
against the pollinia, which, being sticky at their

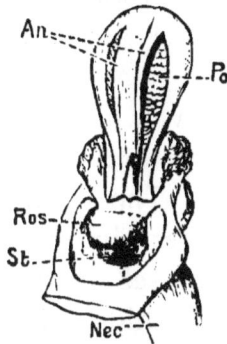

FIG. 65.   FIG. 66.

bases, become attached to the insect's head.   Owing
to the weight of the pollen and the slenderness of the
stalks they gradually lose their erect position and

FIG. 67.

FIG. 68.

assume one more horizontal, so that on visiting
another flower the pollinia strike exactly against the
stigmas.   In a foreign species (*Catasetum*) certain

parts of the flower are highly sensitive, and when
touched by a bee convey the impression to the pollinia which ruptures the confining membrane and
hurls the pollinia at the bee, striking it and adhering
to it where, on visiting another flower, they come in
contact with the stigma.

The various methods by which fertilisation is
effected in the Orchids is in fact more marvellous
than in any other genus. " The complication and
ingenuity of these contrivances almost exceed belief.
' Moth-traps and spring-guns set on these grounds '
might be the motto of the Orchids.   There are baits
to tempt the nectar-loving Lepidoptera with rich
odours exhaled by night and lustrous colours to shine
by day ; there are channels of approach along which
they are surely guided, so as to compel them to pass
by certain spots ; there are adhesive plasters nicely
adjusted to fit their probosces or to catch their
brows ; there are hair-triggers carefully set in their
necessary path, communicating with explosive shells
which project the pollen stalks with unerring aim
upon their bodies.   There are, in short, an infini-
tude of adjustments, for an idea of which I must
refer my readers to Mr. Darwin's inimitable powers
of observation and description—adjustments all con-
trived so as to secure the accurate conveyance of the
pollen of the one flower to its precise destination in
the structure of another." *

In the common yellow Flag (*Iris pseudacorus*) three
of the perianth segments are large and arched over,
so as to form a platform, similar to the *labellum* of

* Duke of Argyll, "Reign of Law," p. 38.

Orchis.   The other three segments of the perianth
are erect and small.   The pistil gives rise to three

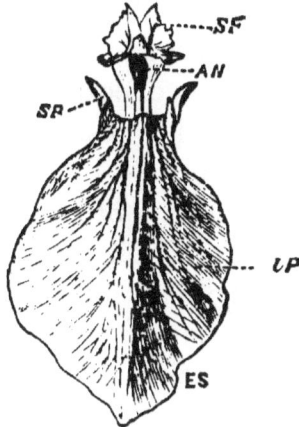

FIG. 69.

stigmatic lobes which are so developed as to resemble
petals.   Each of these stigmas is arched over a large

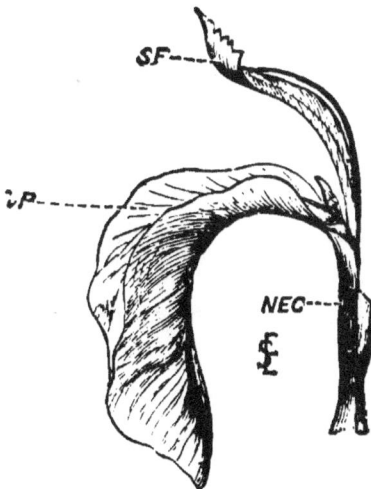

FIG. 70.

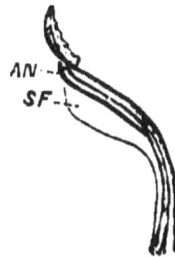

FIG. 71.

perianth segment, and shelters the stamen, likewise
arched.   Fig. 69 is a front view of one segment; SF

is the stigma, beneath which is AN, the anther. LP is the large perianth segment, and SP the smaller. A bee visiting one of these flowers would alight on the platform LP, and insert its proboscis down the nectary (NEC, fig. 70), where the honey is secreted. In doing this its head would come in contact with the anther AN, and dislodge some of the pollen, which would probably be deposited on the stigma of another flower. From the position of the anthers self-fertilisation is improbable.

We are tempted in writing of these wonderful contrivances to multiply examples to a greater extent, for where all is so full of interest the difficulty is what to select. But for the present we must content ourselves with the meagre selection already given, in the hope that our readers will seek out from Nature other examples for themselves. The smallest garden, or even the few plants on a town window-sill, will furnish examples, and there is this advantage about the study—there is the probability of discovering some new facts concerning fertilisation, for until recently no attention has been paid to the subject. Yet now that Mr. Darwin, followed by other able scientists, has called attention to it, facts which previously we could not understand (or if we did understand some of them it was but imperfectly), seem perfectly easy of comprehension. We now know why the Evening Primrose is only fragrant at night, and why the White Campion only opens its beautiful flowers at the same period. Because they are dependent upon the moths for fertilisation, therefore, it would not be any advantage, but rather a loss, to

the plant to be open during the day-time. For the
same reason plants which depend upon the bees and
butterflies close their petals as soon as the sun sinks
in the west. Then, too, observe the manner in which
various flowers are hung on the stalk in order to
protect their honey from deterioration by the access
of rain ; or those flowers in which the honey is not
thus protected—such as the Daisy and Pimpernel—
how they close their petals at the approach of rain.
Such researches have proved an intimate connection
between animals and plants which previously seemed
to lack the most shadowy relation one to the other.
What, for instance, could seem more ridiculous than
the assertion that the clover-crop in any district
depends upon the number of old maids there? Yet
such is really the case, for the clover is dependent
chiefly upon the humble-bees for fertilisation—in fact
one species, the red clover, is fertilised by humble-
bees *alone*. Now it is well known that the nests and
combs of humble-bees are pillaged and destroyed
by field-mice, which in turn are destroyed by cats.
The number of cats in a district is largely determined
by the number of old maids there resident, so that
if in a given district there are a large number of old
maids, there will also be a good supply of cats. If
a good supply of cats the field-mice will be held in
check and their numbers reduced. If field-mice are
not abundant the humble-bees will thrive, and fertilise more clover. There seems at first sight something humorous about this connection, yet there are
many similar instances which Mr. Darwin has brought
to light.

Even the streaks of colour and the hairs on the petals of flowers are found to have reference to the visits of insects; and, in fact, viewed in the light of recent researches, everything in connection with flowers has an interest; and it is with the greatest reluctance that we must now leave this part of our subject.

CHAPTER IV.

PREDATORY PLANTS.

THE analogies between plants and animals are many and remarkable, and have resulted in the breaking down of the arbitrary barriers which of old divided animals from plants. The most able biologists cannot tell you where the vegetable kingdom terminates and the animal world commences. On the border-land they seem to commingle; and some low forms of life in their earliest stages exhibit the characteristics of animals, whilst on arriving at maturity they are found to be indubitable plants. We have previously alluded to the power of movement possessed by certain plants, and we purpose now to give some account of plants which feed upon insects, and which catch their prey.

One of the best known—because the earliest known —of these plants is an American species, the Venus's Fly-trap (*Dionæa muscipula*), which grows in the marshes of North Carolina. It is a low-growing plant, only attaining the height of a few inches. The leaves are given off direct from the root, each being borne upon a long leaf-stalk, which is winged. The blade of the leaf is divided into two halves, fringed with hairs, and provided along the centre with three

highly irritable, short stiff hairs. The surface of the
leaf is also covered with a number of small purple
glands. When touched by an insect, the irritable
bristles communicate the irritation to the lobes of
the leaf, which suddenly close together, imprisoning
the luckless insect. The purple glands, also excited,
now pour out an acid fluid, which has the power of
digesting the body of the insect, which is then absorbed
by the same glands. The leaf remains closed for a
period of from nine to twenty-four days, and on re-

FIG. 72.

opening, is found to have lost its sensitiveness, which,
however, soon returns. It is so sensitive that should
a particle of earth, or other non-nitrogenous substance, be placed upon the leaf, it immediately closes
up, but again opens in perhaps twenty-four hours,
and is at once sensitive. The process which goes
on after the capture of an insect is very similar to that
of digestion in animals. The two lobes of the leaf
form a closed stomach, in which the insect is contained, and from the inner walls of which the digestive

fluid is poured out. When the process of digestion is complete the glands of this artificial stomach change their functions, and instead of secreting pepsin, absorb chyle. The cells of the filaments are now found to exhibit a change in their protoplasmic contents; the protoplasm becomes aggregated into masses of various shapes.

But we have no need to travel to the marshy lands of North Carolina for specimens of such interesting plants. We have growing in our own bogs at home three allied species of insectivorous plants—the Sundews. For the last twenty years Mr. Darwin has been carefully studying the habits of our native Sundews, and other insectivorous plants, and as the result has published a most interesting and valuable volume . upon the subject. More than half of this book is devoted to the consideration of the common Round-leaved Sundew (*Drosera rotundifolia*), a species which may be obtained in tolerable plenty from the bogs in the neighbourhood of London. It is an exceedingly pretty little plant, and very prominent among the bright-green tufts of Sphagnum, where it grows. The leaves are developed from the root, and lie flat, forming a little rosette. They unfold like the fronds of a Fern, being in the early stage rolled up. From the centre of this rosette the flower-stalks rise; the stalk is wiry, leafless, and the flowers white and inconspicuous. The leaves somewhat resemble a spoon, being narrow at the base, gradually enlarging until about the centre, from whence it suddenly assumes a rotund, slightly concave form. The surface is thickly set with long, fine, red filaments, each tipped

with a small knob or gland. These glands secrete a
viscid fluid, which, glistening in the sun, add not a
little to the general prettiness of the plant. The whole

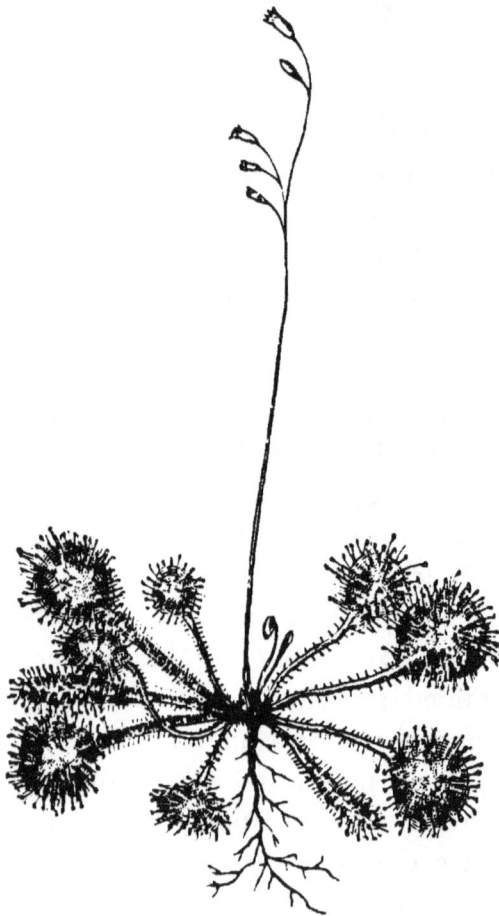

FIG. 73.

leaf bears somewhat the appearance of a flower, and
there is little doubt that insects often come to it under
that idea, but the delusion proves fatal. Mere contact with the sticky fluid is sufficient temporarily to

detain an insect, but to excite the leaf it is necessary that the victim should touch the knob itself. On finding itself detained, the insect struggles to free itself, and in so doing excites the glands. The irritation is communicated to all the filaments or "tentacles," which thereupon bend towards the cause of excitement, and effectually imprison it. Kicks and struggles are useless, the acid secretion is poured out, the insect killed, and finally digested. But the Sundew is not particular as to its food, provided it is of an animal nature. Small fragments of meat placed upon it will produce precisely similar effects. The size of the substances

FIG. 74.

causing irritation is of little moment. Mr. Darwin found that a fragment of cotton weighing $\frac{1}{8000}$th, and of hair weighing $\frac{1}{78000}$th of a grain was sufficient to cause the tentacles with which they were in contact to bend. Such exquisite sensitiveness probably exceeds that of the most sensitive of human nerves.

Recently an addition has been made to our insectivorous plants by the discovery of certain habits of the Butterwort (*Pinguicula vulgaris*). It is, like *Drosera*, a stemless plant, with a tuft of spreading leaves, incurved at the edges, and covered with a greasy matter, from which probably its name is derived. It sends up several leafless stalks, each bearing at the summit a solitary drooping purple flower. It is frequent in boggy ground, but confined to the north. The greasy substance, or "oilous juice," as old Gerarde called it, is secreted by glandular hairs, with which the leaf is studded. The leaf itself is irritable, and the edges become incurved over any nitrogenous substance placed upon it. It

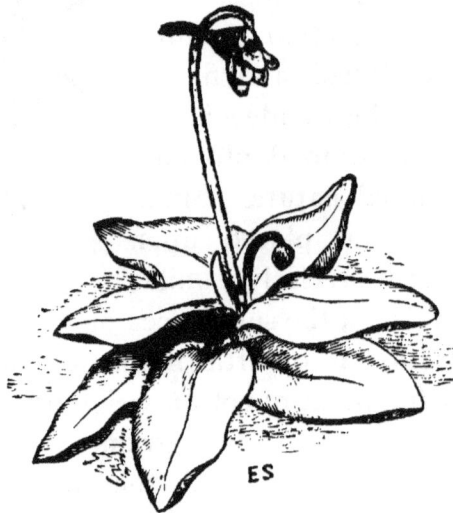

FIG. 75.

is not entirely carnivorous, as some seeds and pollen grains are also dissolved by the increased secretions consequent upon irritation. This fluid is acid, and similar to that secreted by *Drosera*, and after dissolving its food it is again absorbed by the glands, together with the foreign substance it has dissolved.

Another new insectivorous plant is the Bladderwort (*Utricularia*), of which we have three native species. They are aquatic, and delight in the foulest ditches. The plant is submerged, and the leaves very finely divided. The delicate yellow flowers rise out of the water, but the most curious feature of it is the possession of a number of small bladders on its roots, stems, and leaves. These doubtless serve the same purpose as the air bladders of fucus and other sea-weeds, floating the plant to the surface when distended with air; but they have also another function. There is an opening to each, and this opening is closed by a valve which opens inwards only. Through this opening numbers of small aquatic insects and *entomostraca* enter. What induces them to do so is not known; but they enter, and there is no escape. There is no acid secretion from the walls of their prison-house, as in *Drosera* and *Dionæa*—no digestion takes place, but the prisoner remains until death and decomposition ensue, when it is absorbed by the walls of the bladder.

The North American Fly-trap or Dog's Bane (*Apocynum androsæmifolium*) is now tolerably well known as an enemy to insects. In the corolla tube there are five scales which secrete honey, and which are irritable. Insects are attracted to the honey, but on touching—and consequently exciting—the scales, they all bend towards the centre of the flower. In consequence of this movement the insects are held prisoners in the corolla, where they remain for life— which is not a long period. In this and in several other species we shall have to notice, neither digestion nor absorption takes place, and it would therefore seem to be no advantage to the plant to have these insectivorous habits; but the insects really serve a purpose in the fertilisation of the plant, as

E

in Arum (p. 41, *ante*). The Virginian Swallowwort (*Asclepias syriacus*), and the Oleander (*Nerium oleander*), are also included among those plants which entrap insects by means of their flowers.

In a paper recently read before the Entomological Society, Mr. J. M. Slater stated that certain gay-coloured flowers are avoided by bees, or, if visited, have an injurious and even fatal effect upon the insects. Among these are the dahlia, passion-flower, crown imperial, and especially the oleander. That the flowers of the dahlia have a narcotic effect was first pointed out by the Rev. L. Jenyns, who mentions that bees which visit these flowers are soon seized with a sort of torpor, and often die unless speedily removed. Mr. Jenyns also quotes a writer in the "Gardeners' Chronicle," who pronounces the cultivation of the dahlia incompatible with the success of the bee-keeper. The passion-flower also stultifies bees, and bees of all kinds avoid the crown imperial and the oleander, for the honey of the latter is fatal to flies. Mr. Slater did not remember ever having seen a butterfly or moth settling on the flowers of this shrub in Hungary or Dalmatia; and he thinks it important that observers should ascertain whether the above-mentioned phenomena be true, and whether any insects in such cases undertake the functions [of fertilisation] generally exercised by bees, and whether flowers have a similarly noxious or deadly action upon insects.—*Science Gossip*, 1879, p. 164.

In addition to these plants above named, there is a group of others that is really insectivorous. The

Pitcher-plants, described and figured in the following chapter, catch and kill large numbers of small insects, and there is no doubt that some sort of digestive process goes on in the remarkable vessels formed by the leaves, and that the plant receives benefit from its destructive habits.

The exquisite sensitiveness of *Dionæa* and *Drosera* is remarkable, and there is something almost ludicrous in the notion of a plant getting its living by false pretences, for undoubtedly *Drosera* does this. We ourselves have no doubt that insects mistake the round leaf, with its dewy-knobbed red hairs, for a flower, and visit it in the hope of getting honey for their pains. Yet there should be nothing surprising in such mimicry, for it is carried on to a large extent among animals. The Bamboo-insect and the Leaf-insect imitate bamboo and leaves to perfection simply for the purpose of approaching, or lying in wait for, their prey without exciting suspicion. With many butterflies and moths such mimicry takes the form of protective colouring, so as to render them indistinguishable when on a tree-trunk, a lichen-covered wall, or certain flowers. It is the same principle by which frogs and toads, and many fishes, are able to reflect from their skins the hues of surrounding objects, and thus, on a cursory glance, to remain invisible to their enemies.

CHAPTER V.

REMARKABLE FLOWERS AND LEAVES.

WHEN we are acquainted with the structure and growth of plants, there is not one that does not appear remarkable to us, no matter how small or how common it may be. The microscope has taught us that "small" and "insignificant" are not synonymous terms, and a little study will convince any one that the meanest and commonest wayside weed is as much entitled to our respect for beauty as the most gorgeous and choicely perfumed exotic our conservatories afford. But wonderful as all plants—and all living things—are, there are some which stand out more prominently than others on account of exceptional beauty, grotesqueness, or other peculiarity of form. Thus among the Orchids, an exceedingly interesting group of plants, we have one species in which each blossom resembles a fly; others of the same group are supposed to bear a resemblance to a bee, a spider, a lizard, a human hand, and several other forms. Then there are plants which have their leaves or flowers so constructed that any insect of a prying nature is made to suffer for its inquisitiveness by being held a prisoner and killed. But to these more extended reference is made elsewhere in

the present volume (see Chapter IV.). Others have
the leaves transformed into vessels for storing water,
whilst others again have no leaves at all, as in the
various species of Cactus, of which we propose now
to speak.

If we wish to see living specimens of these singular
plants we need go no farther than Kew Gardens ; but
if we would see them in their native habitats we must
seek the neighbourhood of Mexico and California.
Here the Cacti are the characteristic features of the
vegetation.   From their succulent nature they are
peculiarly adapted to this arid region.   Their stems
assume various forms, some being fluted, others
square or angular,
while some as-
sume a spherical
form. Some attain
a great height, ris-
ing like tall fluted
columns to as high
as fifty or sixty
feet. These are the
dimensions of *Ce-
reus giganteus* or
Suwarrow, the lar-
gest species. The

Fig. 76.

flowers are very beautiful, and of a light cream
colour.   Mr. Smith says of this species: "It is a
native of the hot, arid, and almost desert regions of
New Mexico, extending from Souora, in lat. 30° N.,
to Williams River in lat. 35° N., and found growing
in rocky valleys and upon mountain sides, often

springing out from mere crevices in the hard rock, and imparting a singular aspect to the scenery of the country, its tall stems with upright branches looking like telegraphic posts for signalling from point to point of the rocky mountains. While young the stems are of a globular form, gradually becoming club-shaped, and ultimately almost cylindrical, and from fifty to sixty feet in height, with a diameter of about two feet at middle height, and gradually tapering, both upwards and downwards, to about one foot. They are most frequently unbranched, but some of the older ones have branches, which issue at right angles from the stem, and then curve upwards and grow parallel with it. The stems are regularly ribbed or fluted, the ribs varying in number from twelve to twenty, and have at intervals of about an inch, thick yellow cushions bearing five or six large and many smaller spines. The flowers are produced near the summit of the stems and branches, and are about four or five inches long by three or four in diameter, having light cream-coloured petals. The fruits are about two or three inches long, of a green colour and oval form, having a broad scar at the top caused by the flowers falling away; when ripe they burst into three or four pieces, which curve back so as to resemble a flower. Inside they contain numerous little black seeds embedded in a crimson-coloured pulp which the Pimos and Papagos Indians make into an excellent preserve; and they also eat the ripe fruit as an article of food, gathering it by means of a forked stick tied to the end of a long pole." Owing to the exceedingly slow growth, it is probable that full-grown specimens of this species have arrived at the venerable age of several hundreds of years. Dr. Engelmann says: " These trees in abundance give the landscape a very peculiar appearance. As far as the eye can reach in the valleys or on the mountains, little else but rocky boulders and the stately, yet awfully sombre, aspect of the *Cereus giganteus* can be seen. Some species of *Cereus* creep along the ground instead of assuming an erect position. Of this kind is the beautiful *Cereus MacDonaldiæ*, which flowers only at night. It has a bright orange calyx, and the delicate white petals, when fully expanded, measure fourteen inches across. This species is found in Honduras; another and commoner species (*C. grandiflorus*) grows in the West Indies.

FIG. 77.

Belonging to the same class of plants and inhabiting the same locality as the last, we have the well-known Prickly Pears (*Opuntia*), so frequently cultivated in English windows. There are upwards of a hundred and fifty species of them, all confined to the hot dry districts of America and the West Indies. Brazil, Chili, Peru, and Mexico are their headquarters, but they have been successfully introduced and well established in parts of Europe and Africa. It produces its orange-coloured flowers from the flattened joints of its stem. They are succeeded by the thick fleshy, pear-shaped fruits known as prickly pears. These latter are very sweet and juicy, and much esteemed on account of their cooling nature. One species (*O. Tuna*) attains the height of twenty feet, and as it produces large numbers of stiff sharp spines is extensively used as a hedge-plant. In Mexico this species is largely cultivated to afford food for the Cochineal insect (*Coccus*), for which purpose another species, the Nopal, is also cultivated. Several species of *Opuntia* have been introduced into Southern Europe, and so successfully that Dr. Philippi in his "Vegetation of Etna," tells us that "on the roughest lava thrives the Indian or Prickly Pear, of which the large, cooling fruits are sold at less than 2*d.* for thirty. This plant is one of the most useful presents of the New to the Old World, as it grows on the poorest and most rocky soil, where nothing else will vegetate, requiring no attention, and even its succulent-jointed stems are greedily devoured by goats."

Nature is most liberal to us in her supply of necessaries and luxuries; still one could hardly expect her to supply us with such luxuries as toothpicks! Yet even these are provided ready made for us by a species of *Echinocactus* (*E. visnaga*). Some years ago a specimen at Kew was estimated to bear no less than fifty-one thousand of these useful articles. They are—as no doubt our readers have already guessed—the spines borne on the stems of this species, and really in common use among the Mexicans for the purpose mentioned, from which they derive the specific title of *Visnaga*, which means a toothpick. Their length is from an inch to an inch and a half.

Perhaps the most remarkable development of leaves is to be found in those of the Pitcher-plant. There are various kinds of these pitchers, differing widely as to form, but agreeing in their leaves being receptacles for water. One of the best known is the *Nepenthes;* there are about twenty different species of it known, most of them inhabiting the swampy grounds of the East Indies, China, and the Malay Archi-

pelago. The pitchers in this genus are simply appendages to the mid-rib of the leaf, which is drawn out considerably beyond the blade, and a gland at the extremity of it is developed into a hollow vessel with a hinged lid. This "pitcher" contains a liquid which has been found on analysis to consist of binoxalate of potash, and, according to some chemists, muriate of soda and malic acid. The accompanying cuts illustrate the two forms of pitchers found among the *Nepenthaceæ*. Fig. 79 is the funnel-shaped pitcher from the upper leaves of *N. distillatoria*, from Ceylon. Fig. 80 is the ampulla form of *N. Chelsoni*. The rich brown mottling of this form is very beautiful. The liquid serves to drown insects which have innocently sought shelter in the cool vessel, and there is no doubt that their decaying bodies are of service in nourishing the plant, as in the insectivorous plants mentioned in Chapter IV. It is, indeed, there that a description of these plants would properly have come in, but as

the development of leaf is so remarkable we reserved
a place for them here. With reference to this species
there has been considerable
discussion as to whether the
pitcher or the pitcher-cover
constituted the true leaf-
blade, or whether again the
leaf-blade was not to be found
in the leafy portion of the
stalk. It seems, however, to
be now satisfactorily settled
that the latter is the case;
that which appears like a leaf
is the leaf, whilst the pitcher
is merely an enlarged modification of a gland at the
tip of the mid-rib. One
species (*Nepenthes rajah*), a
native of Borneo, has a pitcher
twelve inches long by six
broad, and a blade eighteen
inches long by eight broad.

FIG. 80.

At a recent meeting of the Linnean Society,
Dr. Maxwell T. Masters brought forward a specimen
example of a Pitcher-plant (*Nepenthes bicalcarata*)
from Borneo, and he read a note thereon from Mr.
Burbidge. It seems these pitchers are perfect traps
to creeping insects, by reason of the incurved ridges
round the throat of the pitcher. To get safely at the
prisoners, a species of black ant ingeniously perforates
the stalk, and tunnelling upwards, thus provides an
inroad and exit to the sumptuous fare of dead and

decaying insects contained in the reservoir. The remarkable Lemuroid (*Tarsius spectrum*) likewise visits the pitcher-plants for the sake of the entrapped insects. These it can easily obtain from the *N. Rafflesiana*, but not so from *N. bicalcarata*, where the sharp spurs severely prick if the animal dares to trifle with the urn-lid ("Science Gossip," May 1880). Mr. Alfred Russell Wallace in his graphic and most interesting account of seven years' wandering among the islands of the Malay Archipelago, thus refers to the presence of these plants on Mount Ophir, Malacca : "The height was about 2800 feet. We had been told that we should find water, . . . but we looked about for it in vain, as we were exceedingly thirsty. At last we turned to the pitcher-plants, but the water contained in the pitchers (about half a pint in each) was full of insects and otherwise uninviting. On tasting it, however, we found it very palatable, though rather warm, and we all quenched our thirst from these natural jugs."

Inhabiting the tropical portion of the American continent, from which so many remarkable and beautiful forms of plant-life have been brought to us, we have two other forms of Pitchers, the *Sarracenia* and *Darlingtonia*. In these, however, the pitcher is formed of the leaf-stalk, developed into a thin blade, the edges of which are united. The true leaf is small and forms the cover to these remarkable vessels. Fig. 81 is a representation of the *Darlingtonia californica*, or Californian Pitcher-plant. At the summit this pitcher is vaulted over, and the entrance will be found underneath this vault or hood ; so that

it is impossible for rain or dew to find its way into
the vessel.   We may be sure, therefore, that the fluid
contained within it has been secreted by the plant
itself.   Within the "pitcher" there are short sharp
hairs pointing downwards, and nearer the bottom a
fringe of long hairs also directed downwards.   Large
numbers of flies find their way into the hood and

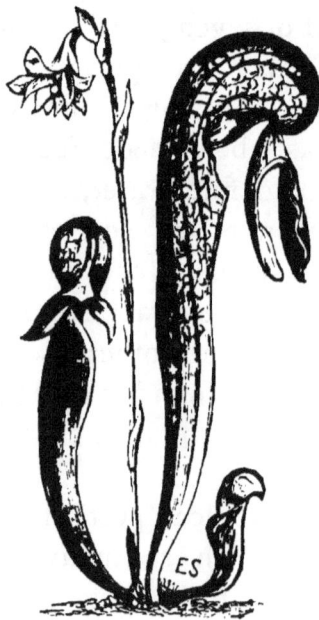

Fig. 81.

into the water.   They can creep up the sides towards
the top, but on coming in contact with the long hairs
are repulsed.   Again and again they may attempt
the ascent, and as often be defeated, until weak and
helpless they fall back into the water to perish.   In
Sarracenia, or Huntsman's-horn, shown in fig. 82, the
pitcher is quite open, partially protected, though, by

a sort of hood, which is the true leaf. Just within the mouth a sweet liquid is secreted which attracts insects. The interior walls are smooth and slippery, and at some distance from the top there is a fringe of long hairs, as in *Darlingtonia*. The insects find that descent is very easy, but the ascent most difficult. If they succeed in obtaining a foothold there is the

FIG. 82.

fringe of hairs to be surmounted, and this is usually a poser for them, if we may judge from the quantity of dead flies always to be found in these pitchers. The plant is found growing in the marshes of North America.

The exquisite little plant shown at fig. 83 is the Australian Fly-trap (*Cephalotus follicularis*), a native of King George's Sound. The pitchers are green, spotted with brown and purple. They bear a close resemblance to the ampullas of *Nepenthes*, and are

FIG. 83.

produced in a cluster round the flower-stalk, which rises comparatively high above them.

Our next figure is that of the *Heliamphora*, a plant found in the muddy places of Guiana. It bears a slight resemblance to some species of *Sarracenia*, with which it agrees in its fly-catching abilities. The delicate nodding pink flowers are borne

FIG. 84.

upon a slender stalk, which elevates them above the pitchers. All these Pitcher-plants are inhabitants of boggy places, and are often brought to this country as objects of curiosity. They may all be seen growing in Kew Gardens, where also will be found specimens of everything that is wonderful or beautiful in the vegetable world.

There is a remarkable genus of tropical plants, which are also entitled to rank as Pitcher-plants, though they are not so called. We allude to the *Tillandsias*, or Tree-pines, which grow abundantly over the trees of Southern and Central America and the West Indies. Their leaves are dilated at the base into a cavity capable of containing more than a pint of fluid. From the channelled form of their leaves they catch large quantities of rain and dew which run into the basal cavity. Thirsty travellers are often thankful for the store of cool water thus retained for their use, even though it does sometimes contain a few dead insects, overtaken, doubtless, in their cups. A remarkable thing about this *Tillandsia* is, that its reservoirs afford a habitat for a water-plant, a species of Bladderwort (*Utricularia*), which is found nowhere else but in the leaves of the Tree-pine. The Bladderwort throws out runners which seek the nearest neighbouring leaf of *Tillandsia*, and there form a new plant, which sends out more runners, and in this way a number of *Tillandsias* are sometimes seen connected.

We cannot boast, among the botanical productions of our own country, the possession of a genuine Pitcher-plant; but that is no reason why we should not make the most of what we have. In the common Teazle (*Dipsacus sylvestris*) we have our nearest approach to a pitcher. The opposite leaves are united at their bases, and thus form a sort of basin which collects the rain and dew. Sometimes as much as half a pint of clear liquid may be found in this natural cup, and pedestrians on a warm summer day might be glad to stop and take a drink from this stately plant, were it not that insects will persist in committing suicide in it. The following note communicated to "Science Gossip," 1879, by Mr. J. Saunders, well illustrates our remark about this plant. He says : "This plant grows plentifully on some parts of the Crumbles, Eastbourne, and during the present season it has

FIG. 85.

illustrated in a striking manner the use of the connate bases of its leaves. The excessive rains of the month of June filled the whole of the connate cups with water; and, notwithstanding the boisterous winds, the stems were sufficiently rigid to resist their action to such an extent as to preserve a good supply of the fluid, especially in the lowest pairs of leaves. On examining them, it appeared that every cup had caused the death of a goodly number of the enemies of the plant, such as ants, caterpillars, earwigs, and such like small deer. There were at least ten or a dozen creatures drowned in the lowest cup of each plant. A few were to be found in some of the higher cups, and in such cases nearly all of the leaves, forming the receptacles, had contact with adjacent plants. The inference seemed perfectly sound that the leaves were so modified as to collect

the rain-water in which small creatures could be
drowned, whose visits would be detrimental to the
reproductive organs of the plant." In former times
this water was collected by ladies for use as a cos-
metic; it also had a reputation as a cure for inflamed
eyes.

So much for the Pitchers! We think we have still
some remarkable plants to call our readers' attention to. We have described plants which possess
no leaves, but we wish now to have a word concerning one that possesses neither leaf nor stem—being,
in fact, only a flower! This remarkable plant is a
native of Java and Sumatra, where it was discovered
in 1818. Imagine the feelings of Sir Stamford Raffles,
Lady Raffles, and Dr. Arnold—who were in that
year exploring the interior of Sumatra—on suddenly
coming across a gigantic flower over a yard across!
Such a production had never been heard of before,
and no little surprise was created when drawings and
descriptions were sent home to England. To give
honour to its discoverers, their names were embodied
in the scientific name given to the flower — thus
Rafflesia Arnoldi. Here is Dr. Joseph Arnold's
account of its discovery:—"I had ventured some
way from the party, when one of the Malay servants
came running to me with wonder in his eyes, and
said, 'Come with me, sir, come! a flower, very large,
beautiful, wonderful!' I immediately went with the
man about a hundred yards in the jungle, and he
pointed to a flower growing close to the ground
under the rushes, which was truly astonishing. . . .
The whole flower was of a very thick substance, the

F

petals and nectary being but in few places less than
a quarter of a inch thick, and in some places three-
quarters of an inch; the substance of it was very
succulent. When I first saw it a swarm of flies was
hovering over the mouth of the nectary, and apparently laying their eggs in the substance of it. It
had precisely the smell of tainted beef." The plant
—for although it entirely lacks stems and leaves, it
is yet a complete plant—is a parasite upon various
species of Cissus—a kind of vine—appearing upon

FIG. 86.

the stem and roots when the leaves and flowers of
the foster plant are withering. The unexpanded
buds of this plant are said to resemble large close
cabbages, and, when open, to give forth an odour of
carrion, which evidently attracts insects for the purpose of fertilisation. This deception practised upon
insects by this evil odour is further assisted by the
petals being flesh-coloured. These petals are about
a foot long, and at some parts three-quarters of an
inch in thickness, whilst the central cavity of the

flower will hold about three quarts! Altogether, its weight is about fifteen pounds. It is several months in coming to maturity, when it lasts but a few days, gradually putrefying, and thus attracting large numbers of insects who complete the work of fertilisation.

There is an insect, well known to entomologists, which stands for hours in an erect and almost immovable position on the stems of trees and plants, with its forelegs held up like arms waiting to seize any insect which may come within reach. This insect is called the Mantis. The reason we have referred to it here is, that there is a plant whose flowers mimic it. So close is this resemblance that a whole genus of plants of the Ginger tribe are called *Mantisia* in consequence. It will be seen from our illustration, which only represents a portion of the plant, that the purple and yellow flowers maintain just the same erect position as the insect, although to those not acquainted with the *Mantis* another resemblance has suggested itself, viz., to a ballet dancer, and hence the plant is familiarly known as the Dancing Girls.

Fig. 87.

But probably the most remarkable flowers are to be found among the Orchids, a very extensive order of British and exotic plants, many of which are culti-

vated in our conservatories and hothouses on account
of their singular and beautiful forms. This illustration
of the commonest British species will give an idea of
the general construction of the flower in this order.
The most peculiar feature of such construction consists in the pistil and stamens being consolidated
into a mass called the *column*. The pollen grains
are united together into masses by elastic threads,
which unite them to a slender stalk (*caudicle*). These

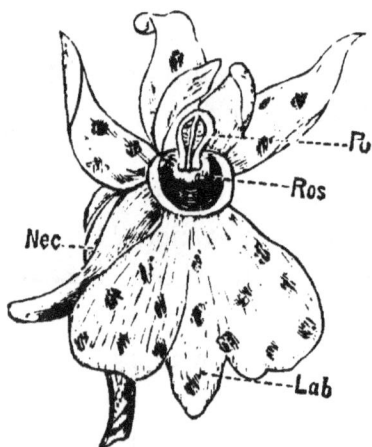

Fig. 88.

pollen masses (*pollinia*) occupy two lobes of the
anther, and are attached by the base of the caudicle
to the rostellum. The stigmatic surface is just below
the rostellum, and at the entrance to the nectary or
spur. The remarkable method by which cross-fertilisation is ensured we have already described (see
Chapter IV.); we wish here to call attention to the
grotesque forms of the flowers. One of our rarest
native species, the *Orchis hircina*, or Lizard Orchis,
has the central segment of the lip very long, tapering

and twisted, so that, with the lateral segments, it is supposed to bear some resemblance to a miniature lizard. *Aceras anthropophora* has a ridiculous caricature of a little man with distended arms and legs; hence it is popularly known as the Man Orchis. But perhaps the best of these "counterfeit presentments" is to be found in the flowers of *Ophrys muscifera*, which remarkably imitate a fly. They are of a purple-brown hue, with a square patch of pale blue in the centre of the labellum. The upper petals provide the antennæ, and altogether the

FIG. 89.

appearance is that of a fly settled on a flower. Old Parkinson says of it: "The neather parte of the flie is black, with a list of ashe colour crossing the backe

FIG. 90.

FIG. 91.

with a show of legges, hanging at it; the naturall flie seemeth so to be in love with it, that you shall seldome come in the heate of the daie but you shall find one sitting close thereon." Whether the latter part of this old herbalist's opinion be true or not we cannot say, but certain it is that the bees are very fond of another species—the Bee Orchis (*Ophrys apifera*)—whose flowers equally well mimic the bee. Two other species (*O. aranifera* and *O. arachnites*) resemble spiders. A North American species is called the Crane-fly Orchis, from a supposed resemblance of the flower to that insect; whilst a British species (*Peristylus viridis*) is called the Frog Orchis, though we have failed to find any resemblance to justify the connection.

All these native species of Orchids grow on, or in, the earth like most other respectably conducted plants, but some of their tropical relatives take to climbing trees and growing from the branches, without any visible means of existence. Some species of *Odontoglossum* are of this habit, though they are chiefly remarkable for the magnificent beauty and large size of their flowers. One species (*O. grande*), a native of Guatemala, bears flowers six inches across; the petals long and spreading, of a yellow colour, beautifully marked with blotches and bands of brown. Another species (*O. tigrinum*) has the flowers spotted with purple-brown, and strongly perfumed with the odour of Violets. A nearly related genus (*Oncidium*) consists of over two hundred species, all of them confined to tropical America, though some cannot properly be considered as tropical species, seeing that they grow at immense altitudes, where the temperature is very low. Thus *Oncidium Warczewiczii*, a native of Costa Rica, grows on oaks at an elevation of from 8,000 to 10,000 feet, and has been found to perish on being brought into the lower and warmer zones. One species is known as the Butterfly Orchis (*Oncidium papilio*) from the appearance of its flowers. The clusters—or *panicles*—of flowers are in some species of an enormous size; in more than one species they reach the length of twenty feet, whilst the flowers themselves are three inches across. *Peristeria elata*, a Central American species, is locally known as " El Spirito Santo," from the resemblance of the column and its appendages to a dove.

In the genus *Catasetum* there is a peculiar contrivance to effect cross-fertilisation. In this species the column bears at about its middle two long sensitive projections, to which Mr. Darwin has applied the term *antennæ*. The *labellum*, or lip, is thick and fleshy, and the bees visit it in order to gnaw its edges. In so doing they touch the antenna, which transmits a vibration "to a certain membrane, which is instantly ruptured; this sets free a spring, by which the pollen mass is shot forth, like an arrow, in the right direction, and adheres by its viscid extremity to the back of the bee. The pollen mass of the male plant (for the sexes are separate in this orchid) is thus carried to the flower of the female plant, where it is brought into contact with the stigma, which is viscid enough to break certain elastic threads, and retaining the pollen, fertilisation is effected."—*Darwin, " Origin of Species*," p. 155.

More remarkable still in this connection is the extraordinary contrivance in a species of orchid called *Coryanthes*, lately described by Dr. Crüger and referred to by Mr. Darwin, from whom we quote the

following :—"This orchid has part of its labellum, or
lower lip, hollowed out into a great bucket, into
which drops of almost pure water continually fall
from two secreting horns which stand above it ; and
when the bucket is half full, the water overflows by
a spout on one side. The basal part of the labellum
stands over the bucket, and is itself hollowed out
into a sort of chamber with two lateral entrances ;
within this chamber there are curious fleshy ridges.
The ingenious man, if he had not witnessed what
takes place, could never have imagined what purpose
all these parts serve. But Dr. Crüger saw crowds of
large humble-bees visiting the gigantic flowers of this
orchid, not in order to suck nectar, but to gnaw off
the ridges within the chamber above the bucket; in
doing this they frequently pushed each other into
the bucket, and their wings being thus wetted they
could not fly away, but were compelled to crawl out
through the passage formed by the spout or over-
flow. Dr. Crüger saw a 'continual procession' of
bees thus crawling out of their involuntary bath.
The passage is narrow, and is roofed over by the
column, so that a bee, in forcing its way out, first
rubs its back against the viscid stigma and then
against the viscid glands of the pollen masses. The
pollen masses are thus glued to the back of the bee
which first happens to crawl out through the passage
of a lately expanded flower, and are thus carried
away. Dr. Crüger sent me a flower in spirits of
wine, with a bee which he had killed before it quite
crawled out with a pollen mass still fastened to its
back. When the bee, thus provided, flies to another

flower, or to the same flower a second time, and is pushed by its comrades into the bucket, and then crawls out by the passage, the pollen mass necessarily comes first into contact with the viscid stigma, and adheres to it, and the flower is fertilised. Now at last we see the full use of every part of the flower, of the water-secreting horns, of the bucket half full of water, which prevents the bees from flying away, and forces them to crawl out through the spout, and rub against the properly-placed viscid pollen masses and the viscid stigma."—*Origin of Species.*

One small group of orchids (*Caleana*), confined to New Holland, possess an irritable lip, which, in fine weather, bends back, and leaves the column uncovered and open to the insects; but if it rains the drops cause the irritable lip to close up over the column, which is thus effectually secured from rain. Similar phenomena occur in *Drakæa* and *Spiculæa*, other species of orchids.

We must now take leave of this interesting group of plants, and again pay some slight attention to peculiar leaves. One of the most remarkable of these is the Lattice-leaf (*Ouvirandra fenestralis*), a native of Madagascar. It is an aquatic plant, possessing tuberculate roots and submerged leaves. For our acquaintance with it we are indebted to the well-known missionary, the Rev. W. Ellis. The remarkable portion of the plant is the leaf, which at first sight looks like a mere skeleton-leaf—one that has had all the cellular tissue cleaned off the fibres—with open spaces between the nerves or fibres. But the microscope shows us that the fibres are really enveloped in parenchyma; and in the young leaves it is more easily seen, as the spaces between the fibres are almost filled up by it. The natives of Madagascar make use of its fleshy roots for purposes of food, as they yield a large amount of farinaceous substance.

We have referred to the largest known flower of Java; and if we, in imagination, visit the rivers of South America, we shall come across the largest known leaf—the *Victoria regia*—a gigantic water-lily, like the water-lily of our own streams immensely exaggerated. Its average size is about six feet across, although specimens have been found which measured twelve feet across the leaf. They chiefly abound in the rivers which are tributary to the Amazon; and Mr. Bates, in his exceedingly interesting work, "The Naturalist on the River Amazons," tells us: "We rowed for half a mile through a magnificent bed of Victoria water-lilies, the flower-buds of which were just beginning to expand." For particulars respecting the vegetation of the districts where the Victoria is found, we must refer our readers to Mr. Bates' book; but we need not apologise to them for giving the following short extract from it :—

"The forest, most of which appears to be of second growth, is traversed by broad alleys which terminate to the south and east on the banks of pools and lakes, a chain of which extends through the interior of the land. As soon as we anchored, I set off with Luco to explore the district. We walked about a mile along the marly shore, on which was a thick carpet of flowering shrubs, enlivened by a great

variety of lovely little butterflies, and then entered
the forest by a dry watercourse. About a furlong
inland this opened on a broad placid pool, whose
banks, clothed with grass of the softest green hue,
sloped gently from the water's edge to the compact
wall of forest which encompassed the whole. The
pool swarmed with water-fowl, snowy egrets, dark-
coloured striped herons, and storks of various species
standing in rows around its margins. Small flocks
of macaws were stirring about the topmost branches
of the trees. Long-legged piosócas (*Parra jacana*)
stalked over the water-plants on the surface of the
pool, and in the bushes on its margin were great
numbers of a kind of canary (*Sycalis brasiliensis*) of
a greenish yellow colour, which has a short and not
very melodious song. We had advanced but a few
steps when we startled a pair of the Jaburú-moleque
(*Mycteria americana*), a powerful bird of the stork
family, four and a half feet in height, which flew up
and alarmed the rest, so that I got only one bird out
of the tumultuous flocks which passed over our
heads. Passing towards the farther end of the pool,
I saw, resting on the surface of the water, a number
of large round leaves, turned up at their edges; they
belonged to the Victoria water-lily. The leaves were
just beginning to expand (December 3d), some were
still under water, and the largest of those which had
reached the surface measured not quite three feet in
diameter. We found a montaria with a paddle in it,
drawn up on the bank, which I took leave to borrow
of the unknown owner, and Luco paddled me
amongst the noble plants to search for flowers, meet-

ing, however, with no success.   I learned afterwards
that the plant is common in nearly all the lakes of
this neighbourhood.   The natives call it the 'furno
do piosoca,' or oven of the jacana, the shape of the
leaves being like that of the ovens on which man-
dioca meal is roasted."—*Naturalist on the Amazons*,
p. 145.

The margin of the leaf is always turned up all
round, so that it resembles a large tray two or three
inches deep.   On the upper surface its colour is a
rich green, beneath it is deep purple.   The nerves or
fibres are very large, and prominent on the under
side.   The larger fibres, which radiate from the centre
of the leaf to the margin, are connected by smaller
transverse fibres, so that the under surface is divided,
or partitioned off, into a large number of little square
spaces.   By this method of construction great buoyancy is attained, and they are thus able to sustain a
great weight without being submerged ; in fact, it is
stated that one of these leaves will support a child
twelve years of age, provided that a small board be
placed on the leaf to prevent the child's feet from
tearing the leaf.

The flowers are equally large and noble, borne on
a thick strong stalk, and, when fully expanded,
measuring over a foot across.   The outer petals are
white, the inner ones of a beautiful deep rose-colour.
When fully expanded these outer petals bend downwards, whilst the inner remain erect, and thus a
beautiful effect is produced.   The flowers have the
additional charm of fragrance.

It seems remarkable that so magnificent a plant

should remain unknown for thirty-six years after its first discovery, yet such was the case. It was first discovered by Haenke in 1801. "Father la Cueva and Haenke were together in a *piroque* upon the Rio Mamoré, one of the great tributaries of the Amazon river, when they discovered in the marshes, by the side of the stream, a flower which was so surpassingly beautiful and extraordinary, that Haenke, in a transport of admiration, fell on his knees and expressed aloud his sense of the power and magnificence of the Creator in His works" (D'Orbigny). But the first specimens seen in Europe were received in Paris from M. D'Orbigny in 1828. These were discovered in the river Parana in Guiana. In 1832 it was again found in some tributaries of the Amazon by a German traveller, and yet it was not until 1837 that public attention was called to it, when Sir Robert Schomburgk discovered it in the Berbice river, British Guiana. In a letter to the Royal Geographical Society he described the largest specimen he met with, the dimensions of which he gave as six feet five inches across the leaf, with a rim five or six inches high, and flowers a foot and a quarter across. Since then living specimens have been received in this country, and so successfully grown that it has reached a larger size even than it attains in its native habitats. Splendid specimens may be seen at Kew, where it attracts considerable attention.

And now we think we have almost exhausted the amount of space we can spare for the consideration of remarkable leaves and flowers ; but before ending our chapter we must take some passing notice of a curious native plant, well known in country districts as Knee Holly or Butcher's Broom (*Ruscus aculeatus*). It is a stiff little shrubby plant, whose chief peculiarity consists in the situation of the flowers. The foot-stalk of the flower is buried beneath the epidermis of the leaf, so that it presents the remarkable appearance of a flower growing from the centre of a leaf. The leaves are egg-shaped, sharply pointed, and tolerably stiff; thus having the attributes of the holly, from which it derives one of its common names. The flower is small, greenish white, and shows up like a little star against the dark hue of the leaf. The flower is succeeded by large red berries, like little cherries. The common name of Butcher's Broom was given to it on account of its former use by the butchers for sweeping their blocks, and it is still used for sweeping purposes in Italy. The entire plant grows to the height of about three feet.

Fig. 92.

CHAPTER VI.

ABOUT A FERN.

FERNS are among the most beautiful and graceful of Nature's productions, especially when seen in their native haunts. To find these haunts we must seek out localities where moisture is abundant, but not stagnant; in the woods, where the interlacing boughs, with their wealth of greenery, form a protecting awning, through which the sun's rays are sifted and robbed of their fierceness. Here in the subdued light—like the light that falls upon the cathedral floor, which in passing through the stained-glass windows brings their colours with it to the floor— here, exhibiting the most exquisite softness of tint and elegant drooping curves, they throw out their lace-like fronds, and fill the air with a fine aroma peculiarly their own. In such a spot, even the despised bracken of the scorched-up common, or the dusty roadside, is positively beautiful, and one of the most graceful objects we wish to see. Or let us seek some deep secluded glen where rocks are piled on either side, with overhanging trees, whose leaves lend grateful shelter. Here, jutting out in myriads from the crevices of moss-covered boulders, and even from the mossy surface itself, large, bright-green arching

fronds, and delicate little rosettes—clusters of seedlings—flourish. Here and there a tiny streak of
liquid silver winds and wriggles down the sides of
the rocks, tumbling and splashing from point to point
in a million glistening tiny orbs that fall among the

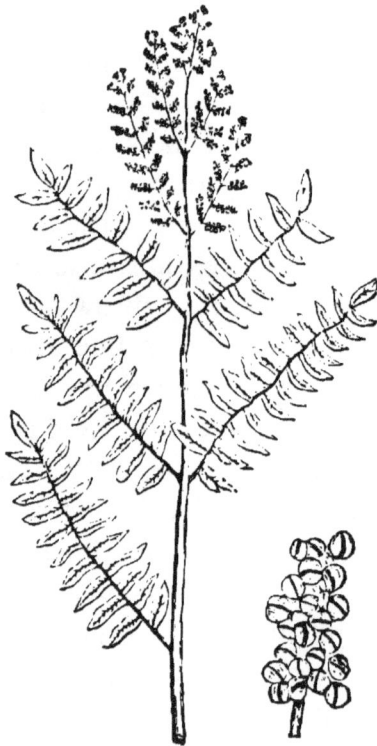

FIG. 93.

moss and liverworts, and keep the fern-roots ever
steeped in percolating moisture. These are the spots
in which they absolutely revel, giving off larger and
brighter, more softly tinted and more gracefully arching fronds than elsewhere. So congenial do they
find their surroundings that scarce an inch space can

be found without its cluster of seedling ferns. In the
deep lanes, too, where high hedge-banks, with their
giant smooth-stemmed beeches, shut out the mid-
day sun, we find them lighting up the gloomy spots.
Everywhere, in fact, where there is shade and moisture, there are ferns; and so great has grown the
attachment of those who dwell in towns to the ferns
that we bring them tenderly home by the roots, and
as tenderly and lovingly care for them, bringing the
soft rich leaf-mould and peat in which to grow them,
carefully shutting out the mid-day sun and giving
them copious draughts of water. The lovers and
cultivators of ferns in towns may now be numbered
by thousands, but of these how many are acquainted
with the structure and early life of their charming
pets? How many, indeed, know the real character
of these plants, their proper position in the vegetable
kingdom? Of course, it is not necessary that one
should have a botanical training to enable him or her
to appreciate the beautiful in Nature; but the botanical training, or a mere rudimentary knowledge of
botany, will enable one to discover hidden beauties,
and wonders not thought of by the mere superficial
observer. Just as in passing along a country lane,
through a wood, or over a hillside, your superficial
observer sees but the big trees and the hawthorn and
blackberry of the hedges, with the masses of stinging
nettle and dock in the ditch below, or the tall stately
foxgloves rising above the dark clumps of gorse on
the hillside. If he mount to the top, he sees nothing
but heather and blaeberry and sky and distant landscape; but to the enthusiastic lover of Nature, who

desires to know more of her productions than those she flaunts in our face, every inch of ground is teeming with wonders. Thus, to the average Londoner, a quiet village in close proximity to woods and hills is bearable for a few days only, when it becomes " an awful bore;" but to the lover of Nature the few weeks spent here will be reckoned by him as among the brightest and happiest episodes in his year's experiences.

But we have been wandering from our fern, which in the heading to this chapter we have promised to say something about. To start fair it will be as well for us to find out what a fern is. We consult a dictionary, and there find, " FERN, *a flowerless plant.*" Yes, ferns *never* produce flowers, and consequently produce no seeds. But we fancy we hear our readers exclaim : " Oh ! come now, that can't be right ! Why, we've seen them, all along under the leaf in little black patches." Thank you, gentle reader, for the correction, but unfortunately for its correctness, no seed can be produced, except as the result of a flower performing certain functions fully described in Chapter III. What you have seen are not seeds, but spores—something very different. If you will take some seed, say a bean for instance, and carefully peel off the skin, you will find it contains a tiny plant folded up carefully. These two halves of the seed are really a couple of very corpulent leaves, distended with starch for the nourishment of the juvenile bean-plant. That little conical shoot (R) lying outside

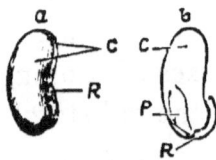

FIG. 94.

their edges is the future root, and the ascending stem
(P) with its embryo leaves lies between these two large
fleshy leaves, or cotyledons (C, fig..94), as botanists call
them. The seed is therefore a sort of bud containing
embryo stem and leaves, but a spore is simply a little
cell containing protoplasm, somewhat similar to those
simple cells we described in our first chapter. It is
impossible in a work like this to go into the scientific
details respecting the relative value of a spore and a
seed, but broadly it may be stated that a spore is
comparable to the pollen grain of a flowering plant.

If we take a full-grown frond from a fern—looking
out for one which has the under-surface ornamented

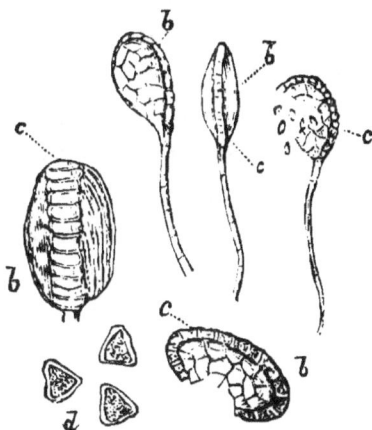

Fig. 95.

by these brown or black dots—and shake it over a
sheet of white paper, a very large number of tiny
brown dots will fall on the paper. Now, if we carefully transfer a few of these to a glass slip and place
it under a low power of the microscope, we shall discover these brown dots to be roundish oval cases of

a pale brown colour, composed of cells, one row of
which has thicker walls than the rest, and thus forms
a band round the edge of the case. This case is
botanically termed a *sporange* (fig. 95, *b*), and the clusters of them are spoken of as *sori*. They contain the
exceedingly minute spores, which are visible to the
naked eye merely as a fine dust. When these spores
are ripe their increased size exerts such pressure
upon the sporange that the elastic ring of cells is
ruptured and extended out straight; a transverse
split occurs in the sporange, and the spores are scattered by the violence of the rupture (*c*). We shall in
all probability observe this taking place among those
under our microscope. Suppose that these spores are
scattered in their natural habitat, say upon some damp
mossy stone, or hedge-bank in a sheltered spot, where
there is thorough moisture. They germinate. First
a little tubular process shoots out from the spore (fig.
96, *b*), and from the under side of that another similar
process is developed and becomes the first rootlet. The
tubular process from which it was developed divides
into cells, which again divide and subdivide, until they
form a tiny kidney-shaped green disc which gives off
from its under surface very minute fibres which attach
it to the soil. This little flat green expansion is known
as a *prothallus* (*d*). On its under surface it gives rise
to the reproductive organs, which are known only by
their scientific names. They are of two kinds, and analogous to the stamens and pistil of flowering plants.
The first of these is called the *antheridia* (*d*, 2), and
are found among the rootlets; the second is known as
the *archegonia* (*d*, 4), and are produced on a thickened

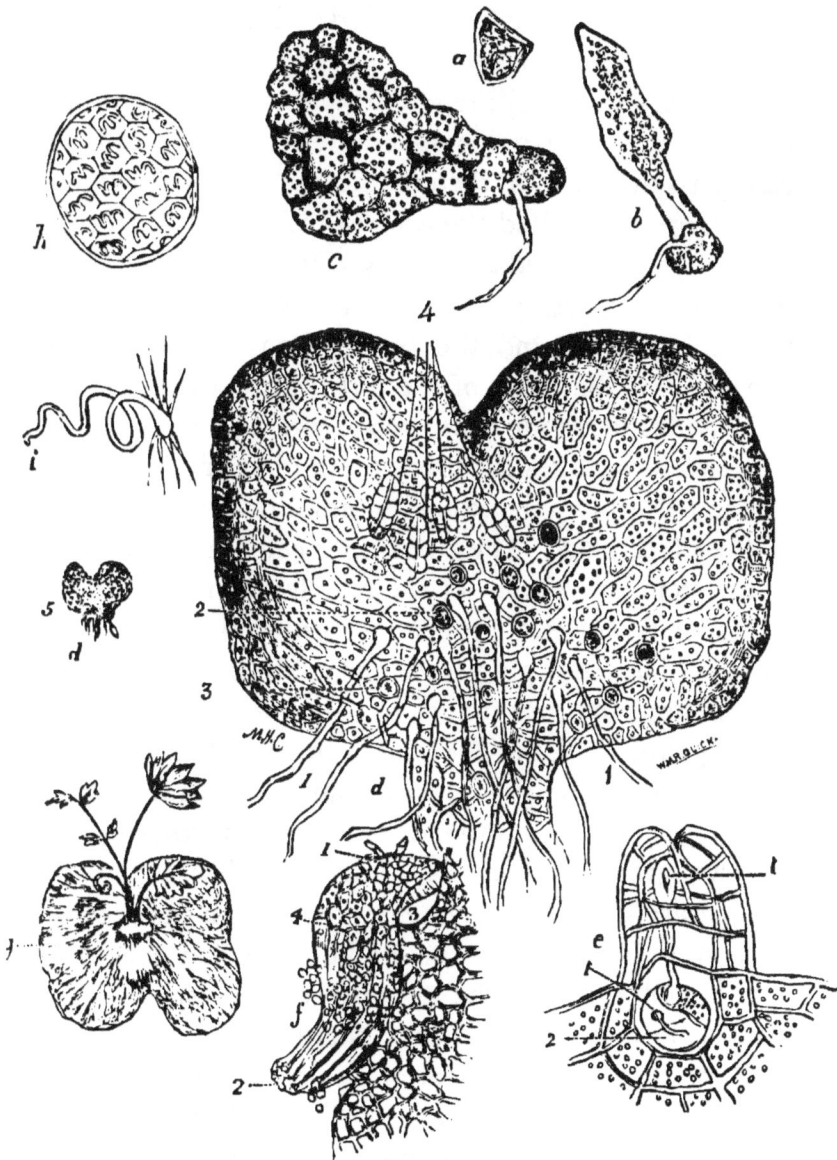

FIG. 96.

portion of the prothallus near the growing point. The
antheridia are small half-round prominences on the
prothallus, which contain a number of little cells (*h*),

in which, coiled up in a spiral, are little bodies thick at one end and tapering off to the other, where a number of cilia are developed. These bodies are the *antherozoids* (*i.*)

The archegonia (*e*) are cylindrical in shape, with an opening at the top; this opening extends as a central cavity to the base of the cylinder, which is occupied by a large cell, called the *embryo-cell* (*c*, 2). Into this cell the antherozoids, when set free, are propelled by their cilia, the protoplasm mingles with that of the embryo-cell, and the fertilisation of the fern is effected. As the result of the fertilisation the embryo-cell divides into four cells, two above and two below. The two lower ones again divide and subdivide until it assumes a plug-shape and enters into the substance of the prothallus. The two upper cells give rise, one to the stem, or *rhizome*, of the new fern, and the other to its first rootlet. Professor Huxley thinks it probable "that the plug-like mass absorbs nutritive matter from the prothallus, and supplies the rhizome of the young fern, until it is able to provide for itself." The rhizome now grows, and sends up delicate little fronds (*g*), and the prothallus, having no further office to serve, gradually shrivels up and vanishes.

Such are the phenomena connected with the reproduction of ferns, and it should be remarked that the fern is not directly the product of the spore. In ferns, as in many other plants, there is here exhibited what is known as the "alternation of generations." The spore produces, not a fern like that it was produced by, but an organism closely resembling the more lowly Liverworts—the prothallus. This prothallus develops reproductive organs which, instead of producing other prothalli, give rise to a true fern like that which produced the spore. In this lies its chief difference from a seed, for a seed produces a plant exactly resembling that which produced the seed.

And now it grows vigorously and sends up frond after frond, until the stem becomes thick and the fronds long and spreading, and bear upon their under-surface spore clusters, like those we have before alluded to. These spores afford the surest method to the tyro for detecting ferns, as no other plants produce spores in the same manner. The leafy portion of the fern is known as a *frond*, but it differs considerably from the leaves of flowering plants. In the latter the point, or apex, of the leaf is first formed, the leaf-stalk last. In the fern the leaf-stalk is formed first, and the apex the last.

If we examine a growing plant of the Common Bracken-fern (*Pteris aquilina*) we shall find it to consist of an underground creeping stem giving off rootlets below and fronds above. In this case the stem is called a rhizome, because of its creeping underground, but if we take the Common Male-fern (*Lastrea filix-mas*) we shall find that the stem, instead of taking a horizontal direction, as in Bracken, is perpendicular, and the upper end is above the ground. In this case the stem will be termed a *caudex*, and a more noticeable example of it will be found in the arborescent stems of the Tree-fern of Australia, &c. It should be noticed that the fronds arise, not from the growing point of the stem, but from certain points at a greater or lesser distance from it. Along the rhizome of the Bracken-fern, on each side, there runs a line, paler in colour than the rest of the stem, and it is from these lines the fronds take their origin. In the Common Polypody (fig. 97),

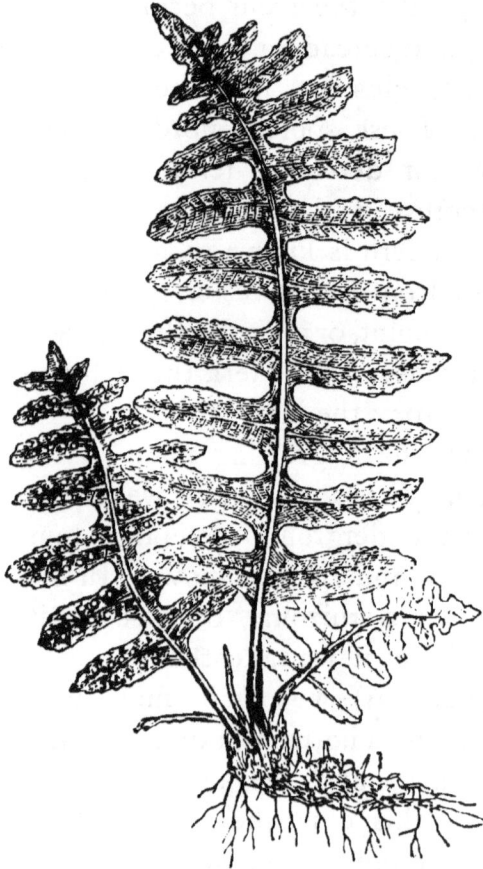

FIG. 97.

which also has a creeping rhizome, the fronds are produced indifferently from the sides or the upper surface. This species, instead of creeping underground, like the Bracken, traverses the surface, and to afford it sufficient protection it is densely covered with thick brown scales. The point from which a frond is given off is called a *node*, the space between two nodes

FIG. 98.

is an *internode*, and it will be noted that in the Bracken and Polypody these nodes are at irregular distances from each other. But if we examine a species possessing a vertical stem, as the Male-fern, we shall find the nodes to be pretty equally distanced, though thickly crowded together. ·

The frond consists of a *stipes*, a *rachis*, *pinnæ*, *pinnules*, and lobes. The *stipes* and *rachis* constitute what, in popular language, would be called the stalk. The *stipes* is that part which extends from the base to the leafy portion, where the *rachis* commences and extends thence to the apex of the frond. The leafy portion in the different species exhibits the utmost variety, from a simple strap-shape as in the Hart's-tongue, to the most delicate lace-like arrangement. In the Common Polypody the frond is simply divided into lateral lobes (*pinnæ*), and a similar division is seen in the Hard-fern, Maidenhair Spleenwort (fig.98), and the Scaly Spleenwort (fig.99), though between each of these there is considerable variety. In the Male-fern a further division is seen, the pinnæ being subdivided into pinnules; whilst in well-grown specimens of the Bracken the frond is still further subdivided, and termed "decompound."

But the varieties of fronds are very numerous, even individuals of the same species often differing considerably among themselves. But all are beautiful, and the very types of gracefulness. Thoreau says: "Nature made ferns for pure leaves, to show what she could do in that line." What can be found in Nature more delicate and fresh than the frond of a Lady-fern? Its delicate appearance does not belie its nature, for, excepting the Filmy-ferns, there is none so fragile. Its slender, almost transparent stalk is very succulent, and if the roots be not liberally

supplied with moisture, it rapidly succumbs, and
shrivels up beyond recovery. Such a circumstance
alone would give a clue to its favourite habitat. It
is in the immediate neighbourhood of water, whether

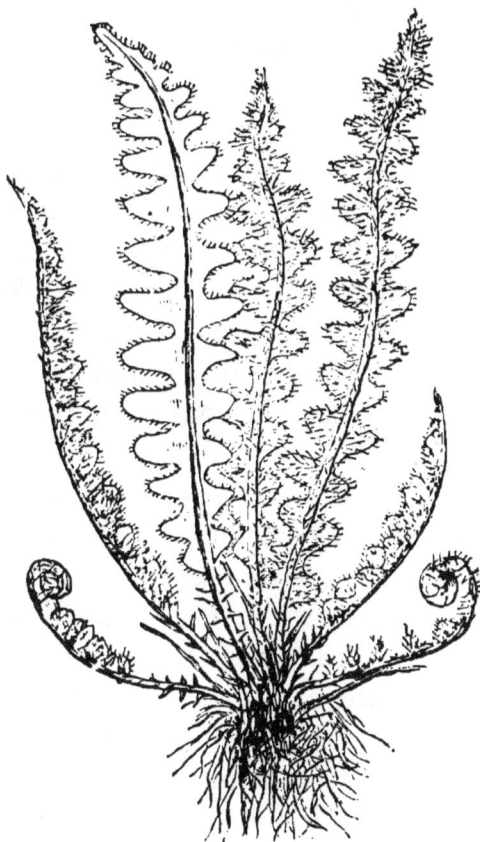

FIG. 99.

it be the percolating moisture of a bog, a tinkling
stream, or a splashing cascade. To see it in all its
loveliness we must—

> " Hie to haunts right seldom seen,
>   Lovely, lonesome, cool, and green."

For—

> " Where the copsewood is the greenest,
> Where the fountains glisten sheenest,
> Where the morning dew lies longest,
> There the Lady-fern grows strongest."

We have in our mind's eye a narrow Cornish lane lined with a profusion of tall gay foxgloves, and strong robust-looking Male-ferns; this lane, which seemed to be used only by an occasional cow, ends in a shady *cul-de-sac*, where a spring of clear cold water flows into a rude moss-covered stone trough, and, overflowing, forms a tiny stream which murmurs through the grass and moss, finally vanishing in the dense bushes which surround the spot. All around the trough dozens of the most beautiful Lady-ferns throw up their frail fronds all jewelled by the glistening dew-like drops, their fibrous rootlets penetrating into the water itself. How those few ferns relieved that corner from the most commonplace aspect! There on that sloping ground, where the rocks just peep above the soil, the slender fronds coil about the mossy stone, whilst above the clumps of foxglove give warmth and colour to the picture. But the finest specimens we have seen were growing nearer London. Within a damp wood, but thirty miles from the Metropolis, we came upon a patch of bog, where one had to step with some amount of caution. Here were Lady-ferns in abundance, mingled with the similarly slender fronds of the Marsh-ferns. One magnificent specimen possessed fronds four feet in length, and here the roots were immersed in running water. Within the radius of a mile from the same spot fully a dozen species of ferns can be obtained, many of them in the greatest profusion. Acres of the Northern Hard-fern crowd each other close among the heather, and from the hedge-banks and the forks of trees hang great clusters of bright-green Polypodies. Here at an altitude of over eight hundred feet you may in early spring find the Broad Buckler with the last year's fronds still green and fresh upon it. But then it is protected well from the cutting winds by a fir wood.fringed with hollies, yet still the situation does seem too exposed to suit this species. In cultivation it must be thoroughly protected both from wind and sun, when its graceful broad arching fronds will have a most beautiful effect. But expose it to the wind, however little, and it will become one of the most unsightly objects, and a libel upon the character of ferns. It is thoroughly suitable for indoor culture, in a room with a northern aspect (which all ferns require). Here it will become, in gracefulness, second only to the Lady-fern, and will retain its fronds all through the winter.

But it is in the counties of Devon and Cornwall that we must seek the ferns if we would see them in all their natural luxuriance and plentifulness. Every hedge harbours continuous lines of Polypody, whilst from the sides of the ditch below fresh-green Hart's-tongues over a yard in length abound. Down the deep narrow lanes, whose walls are built of flakes, chipped from the rocks below, where the trees on either bank, extending their arms to each other across the top, form a cool arcade through which the breezes come from the bay on which we look down from all parts of our sloping lane; here, from every space between the thin flakes of rock, the dark-green shining fronds of the Black Maidenhair Spleenwort, supported by their long wiry black or purple stipides, grow up towards the light, almost hiding the wall on which it grows. If we could only transport a dozen yards of such a wall, with its ferny occupants intact, to our garden in the suburbs of the Metropolis!

With descriptions of the natural ferneries of North Devon, Mr. F. G. Heath has made us familiar in his books, " The Fern Paradise" and " The Fern World." Here is a quotation from the latter work :—

" Under overarching trees, which throw the path into cool shadow, we wind round and round, descending as we go. On our right there is a sloping tree-covered bank, dotted with shuttlecock shapes of Fern; on the left a high bank, richly clothed with grass and Fern, and crowned with trees which spread their fresh-green branches over the road. For some little way the character of the scenery remains the same, but in a few moments we come upon a bend in the road round to the left. Turning round this bend, a gap in the leafy curtain on the right affords us a prospect which compels us to pause. Away just in front as we turn to the right, two hills, densely clothed with a dark mantle of trees, sweep down into a combe. Their sides interlace midway, but the deepest part of the combe is hidden from view. Over the point where the hills intersect each other we get a peep of the sea. As the eye passes midway across the bosky side of the hill to the left we sight a cliff rising sheer from the sea, and in the foreground

of the cliff a wooded bluff descending almost to the
water's edge. As we stand on the crest of the steep
bank whence this delicious peep is to be had, we hear
just below us the gentle murmur and hiss of a stream
of water, which is hurrying down the bed of the
combe to the sea, but which is hidden from sight by
a thick screen of foliage. Down goes our path as we
turn from this delightful spot, and follow its course,
the ferny bank on our left meanwhile rising higher
and higher. Under the shelter of its overarching
trees are glorious forms of *Lastrea filix-mas*, four
feet three inches in length; of Lady Ferns three
inches longer; and of *Blechnum spicant.* Under the
shadow of this tree-covered bank gleams of sunshine
have found their way through the twisted branches,
and the curling leaves are silver-tipped where the
sunny gleams fall upon them. Now on our right
our path passes along the crest of the bank which
heads the combe, whose leafy depths lie below us.
A little farther on, the banks on our left are covered
with Ferns, ivy, and wild flowers, and topped by a
taller growth of trees, whilst the prospect is opened
out on our right between a gap in the trees of the
mouth of the bosky combe, widening as it nears the
sea, whose blue surface is calmly set out below.
From where we stand we can see the rippling waters.
The distance, however, is too great to hear the surge.
But the soft music of the murmuring stream which
hisses as it tumbles down the combe below us rises
deliciously to the ear."—*Fern World*, p. 154.

But in all spots where ferns abound we may find
miniature fairylands; tiny spaces under the mossy

bole of a smooth-stemmed giant beech, where all is moss-grown and cool and twilight ; where moss and lichen and seedling fern are the only vegetation, yet all forming the most lovely microscopic fernery one could wish to see. And such lovely little corners are possible even to the pent-up dwellers in cities. An unsightly shady corner in a narrow, wall-enclosed back-yard may be easily turned into a thing of beauty without expense. It is the fashion for writers on fern-culture, in recommending these beautiful ferns to people who have no means of adorning their homes with the beautiful in Art, dogmatically to prescribe certain materials as being necessary for their cultivation. Among these materials will be found loam, peat earth, leaf-mould, silver sand, &c. A little thought should convince these well-meaning people that such a rigid prescription must tend to defeat the object in view. They wish to gladden and brighten the homes of the poor by the introduction of the most beautiful forms of Nature, but the poor in large cities find it difficult to obtain these materials, and to build up an outdoor fernery in the little back-yard would require large quantities of each. So the would-be fern-grower is repelled at once. But that such substances—however desirable they may be— are not an absolute necessity, we have proved throughout eight or nine years of fern-culture in the Metropolis. The chief requisites are protection from the sun and wind, and plenty of percolating moisture.

We will relate our experience of Fernery construction. At the southern end of our little plot of ground rose a brick wall some fifteen feet in height.

At the base of this we excavated the earth to a depth of three or four feet, getting therefrom ordinary garden mould, gravelly clay, and brickbats. Into the excavation we threw a large quantity of coal-ashes and cinders from the neighbouring dust-bin; these we moistened and beat down into a compact body. Next we threw on the gravel, repeated the beating process, and then cast up the mould, after lightening it with cocoa-nut fibre refuse, a substance which can be obtained retail at the rate of five bushels for one shilling. We now operated upon the broken brickbats, of which we had rather a liberal supply, embedding them in a mortar made by the addition of water to mould, well mixed. For such purposes this makes an admirable cement, which has the merit of soon becoming moss-grown. The bricks were embedded here and there to give firm-ness to the bank; not in any pattern, but just crop-ping out of the soil to afford extra shade and moisture to a delicate species. We also used a quantity of coke, for the same purpose, after dipping it into a liquid solution of mould. Next summer the coke and brick were beautifully coated with moss, in which the fallen spores are now giving rise to tiny seedlings. We also made use of virgin cork to simulate tree stumps, &c.; but this, of course, is perfectly unnecessary. The ferns grow here well, and beneath their fronds we have from time to time introduced many shade-loving wild plants, such as the pretty Wood Sorrel (*Oxalis acetosella*), the frag-rant Woodruff (*Asperula odorata*), the Wood Ane-mone (*Anemone nemorosa*), Ground Ivy (*Nepeta gle-*

H

choma), Creeping Jenny (*Lysimachia nummularia*), Wild Hyacinth (*Scilla nutans*), Violets (*Viola*), and on the highest parts various species of Stonecrop

FIG. 100.—The Adder's-tongue Fern.

(*Sedum*). Mosses will introduce themselves; but it is as well to give help by bringing home from a country ramble a few patches of fruiting mosses, so that the spores may distribute themselves over the

fernery, and, vegetating, lend an additional charm to
the whole.

We wish it to be understood that, in the foregoing
remarks, our object is not to disparage such adjuncts
as the peat earth, leaf-mould, sandstone, &c. ; where
they are accessible, by all means use them, but do
not abandon the growth of ferns because you have
not these materials. We have not space to give a
list of species and cultural directions, but in lieu
thereof would recommend our readers to get a cheap
little work on "Ferns and Ferneries," recently published,* to which we are indebted for the illustrations
to this Chapter.

* Ferns and Ferneries.   London : Marshall Japp & Co., 1880.

CHAPTER VII.

THE FOLK-LORE OF PLANTS.

WHAT a wealth of legend and romance cling to our native flora! There is scarcely a well-known wilding which has not had something to do with the fairies—the dear wee folk who dwelt in flowers, and were always performing good deeds—who trooped out at night to dance in the beams of "the pale-faced moon," led by Queen Mab,

> " In shape no bigger than an agate-stone
> On the forefinger of an alderman,
> Drawn with a team of little atomies."

That they did so dance to the music rung out by the delicate Hare-bells was a certainty, for could you not in the morning see the ring their tiny feet had marked upon the meadow? Such we believed, but matter-of-fact Science steps in and makes the following explanation, driving away all thoughts of fairies from our minds :—"A patch of spawn, according to the fashion of many *Fungi*, spreads centrifugally in every direction, and produces a crop at its outer edge. The soil in the inner part of the disc is exhausted, and the spawn there dies or becomes effete. The crop of fungi meanwhile perishes and supplies a rich manure to the grass, which is in consequence of a vivid green; the parts within the ring, in consequence of former exhaustion, looking dry and parched, and those beyond less luxuriant from comparative want of manure. Thus, year after year, the ring increases in diameter till it attains dimensions of many yards across." *

Who was the miscreant that altered the popular orthography of *Digitalis purpurea* from Folk's-glove to Foxglove? With that alteration all the poetry and the associations of fairyland were taken from the name. True, it is still the noblest of our native flowers, and one that will ever be a favourite with all; but it was the flower which supplied the fairies with gloves—delicately-tinted silken coverings fit for the hands of such dainty folk—hence Folk's-glove.

It is notable that in the myths and superstitions of Natural History the animals are mostly credited with evil or other repulsive powers, but the plants undo the evils wrought by witches, warlocks, and others practising the Black Art. Time was when almost every plant had some marvellous properties attributed to it; and in the old herbals of a few centuries ago a long list of "virtues" was appended to each name. As a rule, one plant would cure at least a score of ills, and the only wonder is that in those good old days folks ever were ill a day, or ever died. But it is with the more supernatural aspect of their powers we have now to deal.

It is not remarkable that the Fern was considered to produce invisible seed, seeing how exceedingly minute are the spores they bear; but in addition to

* Berkeley.

being invisible themselves, they conferred invisibility upon whoever was fortunate enough to obtain them. Thus one of "rare Ben Jonson's" characters complains: "I had no medicine to walk invisible, no Fern seed in my pocket;" and one of Shakespeare's says: "We have the receipt of Fern seed, we walk invisible." But the "seeds" only appeared upon Midsummer Eve, when they had to be procured by holding twelve pewter plates beneath the Fern until the seeds dropped of their own accord, for the plant was not to be shaken on any account. It was held that the seeds in failing would pass through the upper eleven platters, but be held by the twelfth. But sometimes the gatherers were not allowed to hold their platters in peace, for invisible spirits or fairies would flutter around them, and even strike against them, no doubt seriously affecting their nerves. Old Nicholas Culpepper tells us "they flower and give their seed at Midsummer. The female Fern is that plant which is in Sussex called Brakes, the seed of which some authors hold to be so rare. Such a thing there is, I know, and may be easily had upon Midsummer Eve, and for aught I know, two or three days after it, if not more."

The young unrolled fronds of the male Fern were called St. John's Hands, and were supposed to protect the wearer of them against witchcraft and the "evil eye." They were gathered on Midsummer Eve, and worn by the credulous, who also gave them in water to their cattle as a protection from witchery.

The Moonwort Fern must have been appreciated by mediæval burglars and prisoners, for it had the reputation of undoing any lock, bolt, or bar to which it might be applied. Withers (1622), author of the well-known " Emblems," thus refers to it in verse :—

> " There is an herbe, some say, whose virtue 's such
> It in the pasture only with a touch
> Unshoes the new-shod steed."

Culpepper says : " Moonwort is an herb which (they say) will open locks and unshoe such horses as tread upon it. This some laugh to scorn, and those no small fools neither; but country people that I know call it Unshoe the Horse. Besides, I have heard commanders say that on White Down in Devonshire, near Tiverton, there were found thirty Horseshoes, pulled off from the feet of the Earl of Essex's horses, being there drawn up in a body, many of them being but newly shod, and no reason known, which caused much admiration, and the herb described usually grows upon heaths."

A subsequent writer—Coles—thus refers to the above :—

" It is said, yea, and believed by many, that Moonwort will open the locks wherewith dwelling-houses are made fast if it be put into the keyhole; as, also, that it will loosen the locks, fetters, and shoes from those horses' feet that go upon the place where it groweth ; and of this opinion was Master Culpepper, who, though he railed against superstition in others, yet had enough of it himself, as may appear from his story of the Earl of Essex his horses, which being drawn up in a body, many of them lost their shoes upon Whitedown, in Devonshire, because Moonwort grows upon the heath."

The roots and flowers of Violets, in addition to curing a large number of complaints, would moderate anger, and comfort and strengthen the heart. But here is a prescription from an Anglo-Saxon Herbal against that rarity, a talkative woman: "Against a woman's chatter, taste at night, fasting, a root of radish ; that day the chatter cannot harm thee."

The St. John's Wort was, and is still in some parts of the country, gathered on the eve of St. John the Baptist, and hung over windows and doors to keep out all evil spirits, and shield the inmates from storms and all other calamities.

Speaking of the Holly, Culpepper tells us: "Pliny saith, The branches of the tree defend houses from lightning, and men from witchcraft."

All plants with the leaf divided into three, as in the Clover and Wood Sorrel, were potent against all manner of evil. It was a type of the Trinity, three in one. But a clover-leaf divided into four was of far more importance. "If a man walking in the fields finds any four-leaved grass, he shall in a short while after, finde some good thing." Such leaves were good for cattle, but very bad for witches and others of the same profession.

An old author tells us that "the wort that one names betonicum is produced in meadows and on clean soils ; it is good for man's soul and for his body ; it shields him against monstrous nocturnal visitors, and against horrible visions and dreams." The same author, speaking of the Mullein, says: "A twig of this plant borne by any one is a charm against frights or hurts from any wild beast, or any evil coming near."

The Mountain Ash or Rowan-tree was a protection against, and a remedy for, the effects of the
" Evil-eye," witches, and warlocks. Farmers, to protect their cattle, hung branches of rowan and honey-
suckle in their cow-houses on the 2d of May. This
property of the tree is recorded in a very ancient
ballad, entitled " The Laidley Worm of Spindleston
Heughs:"

> " Their spells were vain, the hags returned
>   To the Queen in sorrowful mood,
>   Crying that witches have no power
>   Where there is Rowan-tree wood."

Stumps of this tree have frequently been found in
druidical circles and burying-places.

The Houseleek is planted on the roofs of houses
to protect them from storms and lightning, and the
Welsh peasants consider that it brings good luck.
The Stonecrop, if wrapped up in a black cloth and
placed under any one's pillow, was an unfailing
remedy for sleeplessness, but it must be so placed
without the patient's knowledge.

The Ash was credited with many powers, and
suffered accordingly. The tops and leaves were
" good against the bitings of serpents and vipers," of
which Culpepper says : " I suppose this had its rise
from Gerard or Pliny, both which hold, That there is
such an antipathy between an adder and an Ash-tree,
that if an adder be encompassed round with Ash-
tree leaves, she will sooner run through the fire than
through the leaves : the contrary to which is the
truth, as both my eyes are witness." If a ruptured
child were passed through the stem of a split Ash-

tree it would probably be cured. "The stem of a young Ash being cleft down the middle, and kept open by wedges, the afflicted child, in a state of nudity, was forced through the opening, the mother standing on one side of the tree, and the father on the other. This uncomfortable transit having been twice performed by the astonished and shivering infant, both it and the disrupted tree were respectively swathed up at the same time; and if the wound in the latter healed and the parts coalesced, as was generally the case, a simultaneous cure was supposed to be effected in the child."*

Then there was what was known as the Shrew-ash —but it should be premised that the inoffensive little shrew-mouse has the evil reputation of afflicting with cramp any cattle it may touch or pass over. To cure such cases the good country-folk always had recourse to a Shrew-ash, a sprig of which applied to the afflicted part would effect a cure! But to turn an ordinary Ash into a Shrew-ash required some special preparation. "This they managed by boring a deep hole in the tree with an auger, into which a poor innocent shrew-mouse was thrust alive, with appropriate incantations. The entrance being then plugged up, of course the wretched mouse shortly died, and the tree thenceforward became a wonderful 'Shrew-ash,' and, as such, was treated with the greatest veneration."

Our old friend Culpepper tells us of the Persicaria or Water-pepper—which he calls by another name— that if we put a good handful of it under a horse's

* Coleman, " Woodlands, Heaths, and Hedges."

saddle, it will make him travel the better, although he were half tired before. Of the Devil's-bit Scabious, he tells us : " This root was longer until the devil (as the friars say) bit away the rest of it from spite, envying its usefulness to mankind ; for sure he was not troubled with any disease for which it is proper."

CHAPTER VIII.

PLANTS AND ANIMALS.

IF an argument were needed in favour of the study of botany, no better could be urged, or required, than a statement of the obligations which man, in common with all animals, is under to the vegetable kingdom. There is no necessity, and there is no possibility, of exaggerating this obligation, for man himself, "the lord of creation," is absolutely dependent upon plant-life for his existence. Were all vegetable-life withdrawn from this globe, animal-life would quickly cease, so intimate is the connection between animals and plants. We have seen in our second Chapter how the plants consume the poisonous carbon with which the respiration of animals has polluted the air, and how they give out the oxygen which is absolutely necessary for our existence. This explains why large towns are less healthy than the country— an explanation which until recently the town populations, or, rather, the municipal authorities, have ignored; and so the towns have gone on extending their boundaries, covering with bricks and mortar the surrounding fields and lanes, cutting down trees, and otherwise shutting out the country and decreasing the healthiness of the city. "If a man walk in the woods for love of them half of each day, he is in danger of being regarded as a loafer; but if he spends his whole day as a speculator, shearing off those woods and making earth bald before her time, he is esteemed an industrious and enterprising citizen. As if a town had no interest in its forests but to cut them down!" (Thoreau.) But now men are getting a little wiser, and, even in the mighty Metropolis itself, are learning that the public parks and gardens and the trees by the wayside are a profitable investment after all. Profitable as breathing-spaces, as lungs to this heart of a mighty nation, as spots of beauty, veritable oases in a desert of brick and flagstone. Profitable merely for the sake of the quiet and calm in the midst of a ceaseless babble, or as playgrounds for the little ones. Even the eye is glad of the repose afforded by the masses of quiet green, and altogether we have learned to regard our open spaces as among the most valuable and profitable of our municipal possessions. Dean Swift, in his "Travels of Gulliver," makes one of his characters hold the opinion "that whoever could make two ears of corn, or two blades of grass, to grow upon a spot of ground where only one grew before, would deserve better of mankind, and do more essential service to his country, than the whole race of politicians put together." Though we are not disposed to adopt that opinion in its entirety, we are sure that such a person is a real benefactor to his country, especially if his work has consisted in the wresting of a common from the clutches of a rapacious lord of the manor, to devote it to the enjoyment of the people for ever.

Of such men we have plenty in our midst, and their work may be seen in the free and open spaces which now adjoin most towns; the restoration of them to the people having been brought about only by years of ceaseless activity and continued struggles. Such men deserve to be honoured by their fellows, and doubtless posterity will hold them as distinguished as the winner of his country's battles.

Man by his greed—his desire to turn even the trees and fields to gold, by cutting down the woods and forests without planting other trees in their stead—has done incalculable damage, and in other parts of the world the destruction is still being ruthlessly prosecuted, and the result is a serious alteration of climate. But this is not all. By cutting down our forests, and thus decreasing our rain-fall, we are initiating a whole series of changes. First, we destroy a number of species of plants that cannot live in a dry climate, and with these go a number of insects which depend upon those plants exclusively for their food. The altered conditions, too, may be favourable to other species of insects which prey upon other plants perfectly able to endure the climatic change; but the greater number and increased vigour of their insect-enemies may have the effect of seriously diminishing their numbers. Again, the changes in the insect fauna, effected by the abolition of the forest, will probably have a marked effect upon the birds of the district. So intricately are animals and plants connected that, if we interfere with a species, we cannot tell what effects will ensue from such interference. The mere enclosure of a piece of land to exclude' the cattle from it induces great change: here is an instance narrated by Mr. Darwin:—

" In Staffordshire, on the estate of a relation, where I had ample means of investigation, there was a large and extremely barren heath, which had never been touched by the hand of man; but several hundred acres, of exactly the same nature, had been enclosed twenty-five years previously, and planted with Scotch Fir. The change in the native vegetation of the planted part of the heath was most remarkable, more than is generally seen in passing from one quite distinct soil to another; not only the proportional numbers of the heath-plants were wholly changed, but twelve species of plants (not counting grasses and carices) flourished in the plantations, which could not be found on the heath. The effect on the insects must have been still greater, for six insectivorous birds were very common in the plantations, which were not to be found on the heath; and the heath was frequented by two or three distinct insectivorous birds. Here we see how potent has been the effect of the introduction of a single tree, nothing whatever else having been done, with the exception of the land having been enclosed, so that cattle could not enter. But how important an element enclosure is, I plainly saw near Farnham, in Surrey. Here there are extensive heaths, with a few clumps of old Scotch Firs on the distant hill-tops; within the last ten years large spaces have been enclosed, and self-sown firs are now springing up in multitudes, so close together that all cannot live. When I ascertained that these young trees had not been sown or planted, I was so much surprised at their numbers that I went to several points of view, whence I could examine hundreds of acres of the unenclosed heath, and literally I could not see a single Scotch Fir, except the old planted clumps. But on looking closely between the stems of the heath, I found a multitude of seedlings and little trees which had been perpetually browsed down by the cattle. In one square yard, at a point some hundred yards distant from one of the old clumps, I counted thirty-two little trees; and one of them, with twenty-six rings of growth, had, during many years, tried to raise its head above the stems of the heath, and had failed. No wonder that, as soon as the land was enclosed, it became thickly clothed with vigorously growing young firs. Yet the heath was so extremely barren and so extensive that no one would ever have imagined that cattle would have so closely and effectually searched it for food."

Here we have great changes following on the enclosure of a piece of heath-land and the planting it with Scotch Firs. By excluding cattle, a chance was given to a dozen species of plants not previously able to exist on the heath; the effect of this competition being that certain of the heath-plants were driven out, or existed in diminished numbers. Owing to the appearance of the twelve new species of plants, or to the more vigorous growth of some of the old ones—owing to the enclosure—insects were enabled to exist in greater numbers, and probably there was a largely increased number of species. An increase in the number and variety of insects induces the immigration of six new species of birds which feed upon insects. At Farnham we are shown the reason why the Scotch Fir, a thoroughly indigenous tree, cannot grow unless protected by enclosure.

Speaking of the Scotch Fir reminds us of another change effected by man, by the introduction of foreign species. The Scotch Fir (*Pinus sylvestris*) is the only truly native species of Pine or Fir in Britain, and is held to be one of the most valuable of the European Coniferæ as a timber tree, producing, as it does, the best "deal." But it is a slow-growing tree, and consequently the timber-growers of this country have to a large extent supplanted it by the introduction of the Spruce Fir (*Abies excelsa*) and the Larch (*Larix europæa*), more rapid growers. Previous to the Glacial Period the Spruce Fir was evidently a prosperous native of this country, but in recent geological times it was here unknown until its introduction three centuries ago. To-day it is as common as the Scotch Fir itself. The Larch is an even more recent importation, not having been introduced in any quantity previous to one hundred and fifty years ago. Now large areas are planted with it. So rapid is its growth that Wordsworth called a plantation of it at Grasmere "the vegetable manufactory." Now there is a vast difference in appearance between the Scotch Fir (which is really a Pine and not a Fir) and its supplanters—the former being flat-headed, whilst the latter are conical—and the introduction and extensive cultivation of the latter must have effected a considerable change in the landscape alone of Scotland. But we know that such an important

I

change in the characteristic trees of a country cannot be effected without producing an effect as great upon other vegetation and also upon the fauna of the locality.

What a change must have been effected in our native flora and fauna by the invention of gunpowder! Previously the country owed its victories of war to the bowmen, and they owed their excellence largely to the yew-staves of which their bows were made, and to which the victories of Cressy, Poictiers, and Agincourt were mainly attributed. But with the invention of gunpowder and the adoption of firearms in the army the Yew ceased to be cultivated; the plantations which had been previously devoted to it were filled with more profitable trees, and to-day it is so scarce that the wood for the fancy bows of modern archers is imported from the United States. Previously immense areas of ground must have been planted with the Yew, and the effect of abandoning its cultivation must have been great, especially as it was probably accompanied by an increased cultivation of the Alder (*Alnus glutinosa*), for its wood furnishes one of the best kinds of charcoal used in the manufacture of gunpowder, and in the neighbourhood of gunpowder factories large plantations of Alder are often to be seen.

It is by such circumstances as these that the whole aspect of our country has been changed, and the flora and fauna considerably modified. Think what a revolution of Nature must have been effected by the cultivation of corn! Tracts of virgin forest and moorland were ploughed and dug, and the characteristic plants of the forest and moor exterminated, and with them insects and birds. It must have been a hard fight between the corn and the old occupants of the soil, for no doubt every time the share threw out the earth from the furrow, it brought to the light seeds which had long lain dormant in the earth; and these for a time would choke the corn, but eventually the persevering industry of the husbandman would be rewarded by triumph. But he must continually exercise the strictest watchfulness or the old flora would come back again from the neighbouring wild and take possession of the land once more.

" That moor is a pattern bit left, to show what the greater part of this land was like, for long ages after it had risen out of the sea; when there was little or nothing on the flat upper moors save heaths, and ling, and club-mosses, and soft gorse, and needle-whin, and weeping willows; and furze and fern upon the brows; and in the bottoms oak and ash, beech and alder, hazel and mountain ash, holly and thorn, with here and there an aspen or a buckthorn, and everywhere where he could thrust down his long root, and thrust up his long shoots, that intruding conqueror and insolent tyrant, the bramble. There were sedges and rushes, too, in the bogs, and coarse grass on the forest pastures—or 'leas' as we call them to this day round here—but no real green fields; and I suspect very few gay flowers, save in spring the sheets of golden gorse, and in summer the purple heather. Such was old England—or rather, such was this land before it was England; a far sadder, damper, poorer land than now. For one man, or one cow or sheep which could have lived on it then, a hundred can live now. And yet, what it was once, that it might become again—it surely would round here, if this brave English people died out of it, and the land was left to itself once more.

"What would happen then, you may guess for yourself, from what you see happen whenever the land is left to itself as it is in the wood alone. In that wood you can still see in the grass the ridges and furrows which show that it was once ploughed and sown by man; perhaps as late as the time of Henry the Eighth, when a great deal of poor land . . . was thrown out of tillage, to become forest and down once more. And what is the mount now? A jungle of oak and beech, cherry and holly, young and old, all growing up together, with the mountain ash and bramble and furze coming up so fast beneath them, that we have to cut the paths clear again year by year. Why, even the little cow-wheat, a very old-world plant, which only grows in ancient woods, has found its way back again, I know not whence, and covers the open spaces with its pretty yellow and white flowers. Man had conquered this mount, you see, from Madam How, hundreds of years ago. So man conquered the wood for a while; and it became cornfield instead of forest; but he was not strong and wise enough, three hundred years ago, to keep what he had conquered; and back came Madam How, and took the place into her own hands, and bade the old forest trees and plants come back again —as they would come if they were not stopped year by year, down from the wood, over the pastures—

killing the rich grasses as they went, till they met another forest coming up from below, and fought it for many a year, till both made peace, and lived quietly side by side for ages."—*Kingsley*, "*Madam How.*"

So will the consequences be however we interfere with Nature, whom Canon Kingsley speaks of as Madam How. If we but cut a drain through a wood or common, we shall assuredly interfere with the flora of such district, and when we have done that other changes must follow. Or if we commence at the other end of the series and destroy the small birds— as until recently was extensively done, under the supposition that they destroyed the fruit crop, and there are still farmers and others sufficiently ignorant to follow the same destructive method. Kill off the small birds to save your fruit trees, and what will you have as the result? Insects swarming everywhere; leaves all yellow and riddled with holes, or reduced to skeletons; flower-buds destroyed, and the fruit that has managed to set all maggoty. This is the price ignorant man pays for his senseless interference. Because the birds rob him of a little fruit he snares or shoots them, and as the result loses all that which he had killed the birds to protect a hundredth part of. Recently we came across a paragraph we had cut from the "Daily News," in 1865 or '6—we are uncertain which—but it so admirably illustrates the results of this interference that we insert it here:—

"EFFECTS OF DESTROYING SMALL BIRDS.—The phenomena of the present season are remarkable. If we go for shade into the woods in this leafy month of June we stop short before thickets where the stout young oaks are as bare as in January, or show only the skeletons of leaves, where caterpillars are still searching for some remnant of moist green food. If we meet the country doctor in his rounds, he says that he cannot ride in shaded roads without his hat in the hot noon, because he finds hat and coat-collar thickly strewn with caterpillars, which have dropped upon him as he passed. In the parson's garden the gooseberry-bushes show some withering fruit, but no foliage; and instead, a show of caterpillars actually covering every twig. In the squire's pleasure-garden the ladies are mourning over their roses, almost every petal of which is pierced, or the very heart eaten out by some grub or fly. On any grassy bank where the wayfarer would like to rest there is such a coating of white grubs that he turns away in disgust. If we go out in the moonlight, a dozen cockchafers knock against our faces in five minutes; and we foresee the profusion of fat white worms which will in consequence be turned up by the plough next year. The wall fruit has already received the wound which will turn to decay before the autumn, and the canker is planted in the apples and pears, which will be deformed and seamed, and hard, and without flavour at crop-time. There never was a finer agricultural prospect but for this; but the farmer dreads seeing the mangel leaves blown and corrupted by the vast families of grubs hidden in their sub-stance, and the collars of the roots infested by big cater-pillars, fattening on the sweet juices which he intended for his cows. It is well if he knows that the rooks can help him in this last case, and that they do not want to eat the root, as he once believed, but the destroyers of the root. These melancholy sights are not, however, all that is to be seen. They present themselves in districts where there are sparrow-clubs, and men and boys who shoot a little bird wherever they have a chance. They are seen where a zealous and patriotic rural constable, or any lounger who has nothing to do, presses his services on the residents, to net the ivy on house or wall, to rout out the spaces under the eaves, and make a clearance of every sparrow, finch, thrush, swallow, or other winged creature.

"Where the pest is not found it is where these bird-destroyers are not allowed their will. When refused, civilly or otherwise, they sneer or stare, and find something to do in calling the neighbours to witness that the silly proprietors will have no green peas, nor anything that grows in juicy shoots; that the cherry trees and the roses will be dis-budded ; that only the hardest green currant or two will be left on each bunch ; that the gooseberries will be found sucked hollow, and a full tithe of the cherries and strawberries gone. Such is the spring prophecy; but when summer has come—this particular summer—strangers stop to wonder at a garden here and there where all is green and bright, amidst a series of damaged orchards, and kitchen gardens, and bare copses ; and the paradise is sure to be the place where the birds have been let alone. It is true, the rows of peas have had to be covered for a while with thorns, and some netting of bushes has been required, and some precautions in regard to the fruit trees. It is true, also, that the small birds have helped themselves to some of the food of the poultry, and to a certain share of the fruit; but there is the difference that where the birds are banished the precautions are of little or no avail, while they have a good chance with the birds for partners. This year, for instance, some proprietors have done everything they could think of. They have syringed their plum-trees with nause-ous decoctions to keep off the green fly ; they are sprinkling road dust thickly over their gooseberries, and are dissolving the white grubs into froth over whole banks or plots of grass ; they are employing regiments of children to pick off the caterpillars, paying them by the pint or quart, but they cannot overtake the damage, and are almost ready to give up the contest. If they can find mischief going on in a garden or field where the birds have not been meddled with, they begin to triumph, unless they are aware of the true answer. That answer is given by some lover of rural life—some observer of birds and insects—who says that a single brood of nestlings in the ivy or the hedge has been seen to devour hundreds of grubs or other insects per day, showing that if Nature were let alone, there would be millions so got rid of in a mile (as, indeed, we knew before by the French report); and if, after the insects had been left to their natural enemies, there were still too many, what might not the infliction become if they were left without check? The check ought this year to have been very strong. The swallows came early, the sparrows burst out of the hedges in crowds, the blackbirds and finches have been whistling, and piping, and chirping, as if the world were all their own. But this is only where they are allowed to live; and there are too many parishes and districts where they are not. This is no trifle, and the present season ought to be a lesson for future years."

It is a melancholy picture, but a true one, of the effects wrought by ignorance, and well illustrates the fact that birds are the natural protectors of plants. Insects are the checks upon plants to prevent their too rapid increase; but if the insects should become too numerous, certain species of plants would disappear altogether. To prevent this the small birds are set as a check upon the insects, and that these birds should not increase unduly, the smaller birds of prey keep them in check. Thus every created thing is connected indirectly with every other, and the most perfect harmony of Nature is the result. Man has the power of modifying these arrangements, and uses it sometimes to his advantage, but as often to his disadvantage. He uses it to his disadvantage only because he is ignorant of those laws upon which the whole universe is governed, and by which the harmony of Nature, in spite of its immense diversity, is attained. Is not this sufficient reason why an elementary acquaintance with these laws should be insisted upon?

CHAPTER IX.

UNDER the general term Mosses are included a great number of plants belonging to three separate orders. These are the Club-mosses (*Lycopodiaccæ*), the true Mosses (*Musci*), and the Scale-mosses (*Hepaticæ*), with which are associated the Crystalworts and Liverworts.

Like ferns, all these plants are flowerless, and multiply by producing spores. The Club-mosses (*Lycopodium*) are clothed with leaves throughout their entire length, such leaves being arranged in what is known as an *imbricate* manner, that is, like the tiling on a roof. The spores are produced in the axils of the leaves, and are contained in kidney-shaped capsules or spore-cases. These spores are many-sided granular bodies, and are called *Antheridia*. The genus *Selaginella* produces in addition another kind of spore-case, which contains, instead of the many powdery spores, three or four large round spores known as *oophoridia*. The details of germination in the species producing *antheridia* only have not been observed ; and it is at present a matter of conjecture whether the prothallus resulting from the germination of an antheridium gives rise to distinct organs as in

the fern. But in *Selaginella*, the few large spores
germinate by cell division on one side, and thus produce a prothallus, in which are formed a number of
archegonia. The small spores (*antheridia*) now produce from their interior spirally-twisted spermatozoids, which enter the embryo cells of the archegonia
and fertilise it. This becomes developed into a rudimentary root and stem, with two cotyledons, similar
to the embryo of most flowering plants.

Their internal structure is similar to that of ferns,
and consists of thick-walled cells, in which are em-

FIG. 101.

bedded bundles of scalariform tissue. There are but
six British species, viz., the Fir Club-moss (*Lycopodium
selago*), the Interrupted Club-moss (*L. annotinum*),
the Common Club-moss (*Lycopodium clavatum*), of
which we give an illustration, the Marsh Club-moss
(*L. inundatum*), the Savin-leaved Club-moss (*L. al-*

pinum), and the Prickly Mountain-moss (*Selaginella
spinosa*).   All these are very humble plants, but they
are the modern representatives of giants, the *Lepidodendra* and *Sigillaria* of the Carboniferous Period,
which form a large portion of our coal.   These
Lepidodendra resembled the Club-mosses, whilst the
Sigillaria seem to have been a connecting link between the Club-mosses and the Pine-trees.

   " The Lepidodendrons are without doubt the splendid old representatives of a family now dwindled
down to such things as our club-mosses or Lycopo-
diums.   Now, it is a certain fact, which can be proved
by the microscope, that a very great part of the best
coal is actually made up of millions of the minute
seeds of club-mosses, such as grow—a few of them,
and those very small—on our moors; a proof, surely,
not only of the vast amount of the vegetation in the
coal-making age, but also of the vast time during
which it lasted.   The Lepidodendra may have been
fifty or sixty feet high.   There is not a Lycopodium
in the world now, I believe, five feet high.   But the
club-mosses are now, in these islands and elsewhere,
lovers of wet and peaty soils, and so may their huger
prototypes have been in the old forests of the coal"
(Kingsley*).

   The spores of existing species form an unimportant
article of commerce, under the popular name of
"vegetable lightning;" they are highly inflammable,
and are used for the purpose of producing stage
lightning, hence the name.   They are also used for
coating pills, and are probably well known to young-

* Town Geology, p. 128.

sters of an experimental turn of mind, on account of their extreme resistance to damp. If the hand be rubbed over with these spores it may be plunged into water without wetting the flesh. One species (*L. alpinum*) is used in Iceland for dyeing wool yellow.

The true mosses (*Musci*) differ from the Club-mosses in possessing *no vessels*,—they are *entirely cellular* in their structure. They are either erect or creeping plants; if the former they are unbranched, if the latter branched. At the apex of their stems they bear the reproductive organs—*Archegonia* and *Antheridia*. When the archegonium has been fertilised by an antherozoid, it develops its nucleus, which grows into an urn or capsule, covered by the *calyptra*, which is the remains of the archegonium. Within the capsule the spores are contained in the form of exceedingly fine powder, which may be carried great distances by the wind. Fig. 102 shows the *calyptra* covering the *sporange*, shown in fig. 103. *Op* is the *operculum* or lid, which opens when the spores are ripe and sets them free. In many species the mouth of the *sporange* is fringed with beautiful little teeth, which form what is known as the *peristome*. Fig. 104 represents the *antheridia* (*an*), together with two cells from the same containing the curled-up *antherozoids* by which the *archegonia* are fertilised. They adhere to any damp surface, whether it be soil, stone, or wood, and soon germinate, giving rise to a thin felt-like mass of green threads. From this mass the plant springs, and in turn bears the reproductive organs.

Mosses have no stomata on their leaves or stem—though sometimes they occur upon the capsule—but it is evident that they absorb gases like other plants. This they probably effect through the walls of the cells composing their substance.

FIG. 103.

FIG. 102.

FIG. 104.

Mosses are to be found everywhere. "The hard-beaten sides of footpaths, the loose crumbling matter at the base of rocks, the sand by the seashore, the rich moist banks of ditches, the grassy meadow, the naked clay, the deep recesses of woods, the peaty soil of heaths and moors, the damp margins of pools or swamps, and wet boggy ground, have their own appropriate species; not to mention the variety of mosses which are truly aquatic, whether in rapid streams or quiet waters. The mud-capped walls which are so frequent in oölitic districts, produce always a multitude of species, some of them of rare occurrence elsewhere, while the little mounds made by ants are sometimes extremely productive. The *Phasca* seems to luxuri-

ate especially in fallow fields, where the soil is thin
and not retentive of moisture, especially in calcareous
districts.   Within a square yard half-a-dozen species
may sometimes be found when these conditions
exist.   Though at a moderate distance from the sea
a variety of species may occasionally be found in
great perfection, there are very few which, like *Schis-
tidium maritimum,* choose by preference situations
constantly exposed to the spray of salt water " (Berkeley).

On the fernery they should be encouraged, not
only for the sake of their own beauty, which is great,
but as helping to prevent the excessive evaporation
of moisture from the soil, and conducting the moisture from the atmosphere.   They form a suitable
nidus for fern-spores to fall upon, affording them the
requisite conditions to induce germination.   They
also serve to prepare hard soils for more deeply-root-
ing plants, and for this reason are among the most
valuable of Nature's pioneers, covering the hard rocks
with a soft coating of delicate green.   Their tiny
rootlets break up the surface of the rock, and their
dead bodies gradually form a thick stratum of vegetable mould, still covered by the younger living
individuals.   Here the wind-borne seeds of the giant
pines and firs find a resting-place, and, germinating,
send their long roots down into the fissures of the
rock for support, and absorb their nourishment from
the moss-made mould.   And in this way Nature
covers up the bare rocks with the most beautiful of
mantles, that of living greenery, and always the
mosses and liverworts and lichens are the humble

plants which prepare a soil for the larger growths of oak and pine.

The Scale-mosses (*Jungermanniaceæ*) closely resemble the true mosses (*Musci*) at a superficial glance, but there are many points in which they differ when closely examined. In the Scale-mosses the sporangia (*Sp*, figs. 105, 107, 108), when ripe, split *down the sides* to allow the spores to escape, whilst

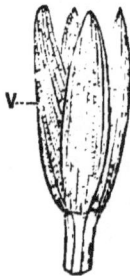

V---

FIG. 105.

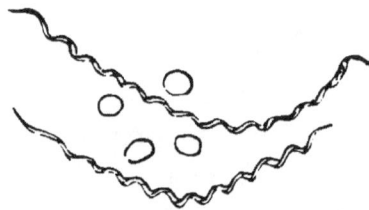

FIG. 106.

in *Musci*, as we have seen, they open at the top with a lid. This sporange rises from a *calyptra* or hood

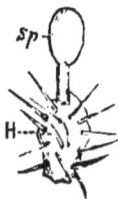

sp---

sp---

H---

FIG. 107.

Sp---

cax---

FIG. 108.

(H, fig. 107), which is itself enclosed in a *calyx* (*cax*, fig. 108). The spores are mixed up with curious spirally - twisted threads (*elaters*, fig. 106). The capsule or sporange splits into four valves (V, fig. 105), which fall down and allow the dispersion of the spores.

A few of these plants have no distinction between stem and leaf, but have a horizontal frond; but by far the greater number have distinct stem and leaves, like the mosses, though the leaves are of a more delicate texture, and lack the mid-rib which many of the mosses possess. The germination of the spores is similar to that of mosses.

The Liverworts (*Marchantiaceæ*) have no distinct stem or leaves, but consist of a flat, horizontal cellular frond, attached by tiny rootlets from the under surface. There are but nine British species, the most plentiful of which is the Common Liverwort (*Marchantia polymorpha*), which will serve to illustrate the order. It is very common in all moist

Fig. 109.

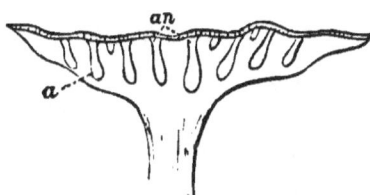

Fig. 110.

situations, its dull green fronds covering patches of earth. The organs of reproduction are borne upon stalks. The antheridia and archegonia are produced on separate plants. The antheridia receptacle is shown in fig. 109. It is slightly concave on the upper surface, and studded with the openings of the antheridia, which are embedded in its substance (fig. 110, section). They contain the antherozoids, which, on being set free, enter and fertilise the archegonia, which give rise to the sporangia shown in fig. 111. The spore cases are arranged on the under surface

K

of the receptacle, and contain spores mixed with elaters, as in the Scale-mosses. The fronds also bear upon their upper surface little cups containing spore-like bodies, which are really buds, or *gemmæ*, and capable of developing into perfect plants. The purpose of these buds is evidently to perpetuate the plant when it is growing under conditions unfavourable to the production of spores.

FIG. 111.

Formerly this species had a great reputation for its supposed medicinal virtues. Old Culpepper says of it: "It is under the dominion of Jupiter, and under the sign Cancer. It is a singular good herb for all the diseases of the liver, both to cool and cleanse it, and helpeth the inflammations in any part, and the yellow jaundice likewise: Being bruised and boiled in small beer, and drunk, it cooleth the heat of the liver and kidneys."

The remaining order of this group of plants is known as the *Ricciaceæ* or Crystalworts. It is a very small order, containing only six British species. They are somewhat similar in structure to the Liverworts, but simpler. The spore cases are not stalked, but borne upon the surface of the frond, or embedded in it, as in fig. 112. The spores are *not* mixed with elaters in this group, neither do the spore cases split into valves.

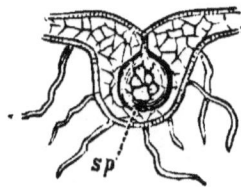

FIG. 112.

The Lichens are more nearly allied to the *Fungi*,

though in form many of them resemble some of the Liverworts. Yet though allied to the *Fungi*, there is no close relation to them. Fungi derive their nourishment from the substances upon which they grow. Not so Lichens. Their food is absorbed from the atmosphere, and it may be taken as a general rule that where Lichens grow the atmosphere is pure, for any impurity kills them. They have been observed to disappear entirely from districts where they formerly occurred in great abundance ; and such disappearance has been entirely due to the pollution of their atmosphere by the growth of a manufacturing town, the establishment of a colliery, or other smoke-producing industry. Mr. W. Johnson, in a recent volume of "Science Gossip," gives an instance of the disappearance of a species from the woods of Gibside, Durham. "In Winch's 'Flora of Northumberland,' published in the Trans. Nat. Hist. Society of Northumberland and Durham, 1832, mention is made of a number of lichens growing in woods at Gibside, Durham. Amongst the plants enumerated is *Evernia prunastri*, said to be in fructification in Gibside Woods. As I have never had the pleasure of gathering this species in fruit in any part of North Durham, or the west and south of Northumberland (which I have more or less searched) I went out to Gibside in the spring to see if I could find the above lichen. Gibside is some seven miles from Newcastle to the south-west. The hall is beautifully placed on the Derwent. The surrounding woods run back on to Whickham Fell. On the latter I found one or two forms of *Callema*, and what seemed to be *Peltigera malacea*, but it was not in fruit, and a few of the commoner forms of *Lecanora* and *Lecidea*. Gibside Woods, barring the atmosphere, are favourable enough for the growth of fructiculose and foliaceous lichens, but for any of these forms I searched in vain. Not a trace of the series *Ramolodei* could I find. The trees were as barren of *Usnea*, *Ramalina*, and *Evernia* as if they had never known them, and I might say of almost every other form. I found here and there on an old fir a few barren patches of the thallus of some *Calicium*; and I noticed a few forms of *Lecanora* and *Lecidea* by the river side.

"The lichens which flourished here in the fine condition spoken of by Winch have perished, and this evidently from the pollution of the atmosphere by the smoke and fumes from the Tyneside, and the collieries of the surrounding district. Though these are a considerable distance from Gibside, yet the deleterious elements travel on the wind, for the trees have that dusky coating on their trunks and branches which is peculiar to trees bordering a town, and which is fatal to lichen-growth." *

The development of these plants is exceedingly slow, and they take years to come to maturity, owing greatly to the fact that their growth is suspended during dry weather. There is little necessity to describe them, as all are acquainted with their grey or yellow incrustations on the rocks of the mountain side, the trunks of trees, and even upon brick walls. But beneath this sober coat of grey they possess a

* Science Gossip, 1879, p. 217.

layer of green cells, which are capable, when set free, of giving rise to new individuals. These green cells are known as *gonidia* (fig. 113, G), and concerning them a humorous theory was promulgated a few years ago, but met with the ridicule it deserved. Professor Schwendener, the author of this theory, believed that these *gonidia* were neither more nor less than *algæ*—little plants allied to the *protococcus* described in Chapter I.—which had been captured by a fungus, and made to provide nutriment for their captor. But we will give the learned Professor's own words :—

"As the result of my researches, all these growths are not simple plants—not individuals in the usual sense of the term; they are rather colonies, which consist of hundreds and thousands of individuals, of which, however, only one acts as master, while the others in perpetual captivity provide nourishment for themselves and their master. This master is a fungus of the order *Ascomycetes*, a parasite which is accustomed to live upon the work of others ; its slaves are green algæ, which it has sought out, or indeed caught hold of, and forced into its service. It surrounds them, as a spider does its prey, with a fibrous net of narrow meshes, which is gradually converted into an impenetrable covering. While, however, the spider sucks its prey, and leaves it lying dead, the fungus, incites the algæ taken in its net to more rapid activity ; nay, to more vigorous increase."

It is unnecessary here to state the facts which prevent the acceptance of this theory : we, in fact, should not have thought it necessary to allude to the subject

were it not that, quite recently, we read in an elementary botany, intended for use in schools, that
" Lichens are true Fungi ; they are found preying
upon families of Algæ. . . . When the Algæ are freed
from the Fungi which imprisoned them, their growth
proceeds ; but the Fungi cannot live without the
Algæ nourishing them." Nothing could be more
absurd than the notion of teaching children as facts
that which has been termed " sensational romance "
by every well-known practical fungologist and lichen-
ologist. The enquiring reader who is curious to know
what has been said of this theory, *pro* and *con*, should
see an article by the Rev. J. M. Crombie in the "Popular Science Review," July
1874, also one by Mr.
W. Archer in " Quarterly
Journal of Microscopical
Science," vol. xiii. p. 217.

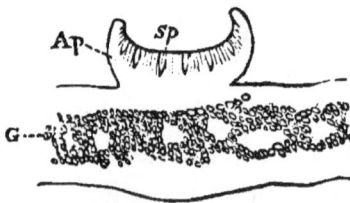

FIG. 113.

What we have in the
Liverworts termed a frond,
in the Lichens is known
as a *thallus.* Fig. 113 is a transverse action of a
thallus, or, rather, a portion of a thallus surmounted
by an *apothecium* (*Ap*). This latter is analogous to
the archegonium in certain other plants considered in
the present Chapter. It contains a large number of
sporangia embedded in it (*Sp*). Other organs analogous to antheridia are found embedded in the thallus,
and opening on the surface by pores. They contain
little filamentous bodies, the *Spermatia*, like antherozoids. Fig. 114 represents a lichen popularly known
as the Cup-moss (*Cenomyce pyxidata*).

With the exception of *Diatomaceæ*, lichens can endure a greater amount of cold than any other plants. *Claydonia rangiferina* or Rein-deer Moss, so common on some of our highest heaths, is exceedingly abundant at the Poles, and forms the staple food of the animal from which it gets its name. The well-known Iceland Moss (*Cetraria islandica*) is a lichen and edible. A few species are used in medicine; more are of importance for dyeing purposes. With these few exceptions they have little economical value.

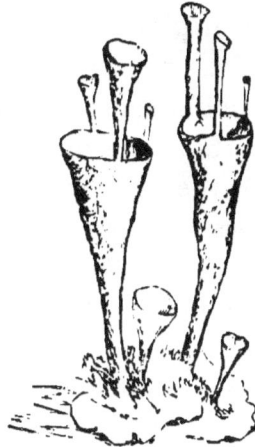

Fig. 114.

We cannot better conclude this Chapter than by giving a quotation from Ruskin :—

" Meek creatures! the first mercy of the earth, veiling with hushed softness its dintless rocks; creatures full of pity, covering with strange and tender honour the scarred disgrace of ruin — laying quiet finger on the trembling stones to teach them rest. No words, that I know of, will say what these mosses are. None are delicate enough, none perfect enough, none rich enough. How is one to tell of the rounded bosses of furred and beaming green — the starred divisions of rubied bloom, fine filmed, as if the Rock Spirits could spin porphyry as we do glass — the traceries of intricate silver, and fringes of amber, lustrous, arborescent, burnished through every fibre into fitful brightness and glossy traceries of silken change, yet all subdued and pensive, and framed for simplest, sweetest offices of grace? They will not be gathered, like the flowers, for chaplet or love-token; but of these the wild bird will make its nest, and the wearied child its pillow.

"And, as they are the earth's first mercy, so they are its last gift to us. When all other service is vain, from plant and tree, the soft mosses and grey lichen take up their watch by the headstone. The woods, the blossoms, the gift-bearing grasses, have done their parts for a time, but these do service for ever. Trees for the builder's yard, flowers for the bride's chamber, corn for the granary, moss for the grave.

"Yet as in one sense the humblest, in another they are the most honoured of the earth-children. Unfading as motionless, the worm frets them not, and the autumn wastes them not. Strong in lowliness, they neither blanch in heat nor pine in frost. To them, slow-fingered, constant-hearted, is entrusted the weaving of the dark eternal tapestries of the hills; to them, slow-pencilled, iris-eyed, the tender framing of their endless imagery. Sharing the stillness of the unimpassioned rock, they share also its endurance; and while the winds of departing spring scatter the white hawthorn blossom like drifted snow, and summer dims on the parched meadow the drooping of its cowslip-gold—far above, among the mountains, the silver lichen-spots rest, star-like, on the stone; and the gathering orange stain upon the edge of yonder western peak reflects the sunset of a thousand years."

CHAPTER X.

THE old astrologers, who professed to read in the stars and planets all about the affairs of this earth, believed that an intimate relation subsisted between plants and planets, perhaps owing to the fact that there is but the difference of an *e* between them. According to these worthy gentlemen every species of plant was an unfailing specific for a certain number of diseases. It is true that their arrangement of maladies and medicine was purely theoretical, but they worked by the doctrine of signatures—that is, every plant was supposed to bear a sign of its own virtues. Thus, any plant which had heart-shaped leaves would be "a singular good medicine for the heart." But many plants do not possess leaves resembling organs of the human body, still many possessed names which connected them therewith. Thus the pretty little Eyebright, in all probability had its name bestowed on account of its bright little flowers peeping out like eyes from the dark background afforded by its leaves. Enough that it is called Eyebright—it must therefore be good for the eyes. Or if it had nothing in its name to connect it with suffering members, there would certainly be something to connect it with the gods and goddesses whose names the planets bear. Thus the Lady-fern would naturally be under the dominion of Venus, and all other plants would be equally under the care and protection of other planets.

The perusal of one of the old "Herbals," which set forth the supposed virtues of plants, and from which our ancestors prepared their "simples," affords considerable amusement to the modern botanist. One of the best known of these is "The English Physician, by Nicholas Culpepper, Gent., Student in Physic and Astrology," a book which has doubtless been the means of killing many credulous persons in the past. The author classifies his plants in the simplest manner possible, alphabetically, and commences with the Woody Nightshade, which he terms *Amara dulcis.*

"It bears many leaves; they grow in no order at all, at least in no regular order. It is under the planet Mercury, and a notable herb of his also, if it be rightly gathered under his influence. It is excellent good to remove witchcraft both in man and beasts, as also all sudden diseases whatsoever. Being tied round about the neck, it is one of the admirablest remedies for the vertigo or dizziness in the head that is; and that is the reason (as Tragus saith) the people in Germany commonly hang it about their cattle's necks, when they fear any such evil hath betided them." Then follows a list of other ailments for which the plant is a sovereign remedy, and our astrologer remarks, "And when you find good by this remember me."

Of the All Heal he says: "It is under the dominion of Mars, hot, biting, and cholerick; and remedies what evils Mars afflicts the body of man with, by sympathy, as viper's flesh attracts poison, and the loadstone iron."

The Alkanet is "under the dominion of Venus, and indeed one of her darlings, though somewhat hard to come by." "Dioscorides sa th, it helps such as are bitten by a venomous beast, whether it be taken inwardly or applied to the wound; nay, he saith further, if any one that hath newly eaten it, do but spit into the mouth of a serpent, the serpent instantly dies."

He tells us of the Adder's-tongue fern: "It is an herb under the dominion of the Moon and Cancer, and therefore, if the disease be caused by the evil influence of Saturn in any part of the body governed by the moon, or under the dominion of Cancer, this herb cures it by sympathy. What parts of the body are under each planet and sign, and also what disease, may be found in my astrological judgment of diseases." He further tells his readers that similar particulars concerning "the internal work of nature in the body of man may be found in my *Ephemeris* for the year 1651. In both which you shall find the chaff of authors blown away by the fame of Dr. Reason, and nothing but rational truths left for the ingenious to feed upon. Lastly, to avoid blotting paper with one thing many times, and also to ease your purses in the price of the book, and withal to make you studious in physic, you have at the latter end of the book the way of preserving all herbs either in juice, conserve, oil, ointment or plaster, electuary, pills or troches."

"Agrimony is an herb under Jupiter, and the sign Cancer; and strengthens those parts under the planet and sign, and removes diseases in them by sympathy, if they happen in any part of the body governed by Jupiter, or under the signs Cancer, Saggitary, or Pisces, and therefore must needs be good for the gout, either used outwardly in oil or ointment, or inwardly in an electuary, or syrup, or concerted juice." He anticipates the incredulous reader, and says: "I cannot stand to give you a reason in every herb, why it cureth such diseases; but if you please to peruse my judgment in the herb Wormwood, you shall find them there, and it will be well worth your while to consider it in every herb, you shall find them true throughout the book."

Upon this hint we turn to Wormwood, where we find the following:—"Will you give me leave to be critical a little? I must take leave: Wormwood is an herb of Mars, and if Pontanus say otherwise he is beside the bridge; I prove it thus: What delights in martial places is a martial herb; but Wormwood delights in martial places (for about forges and iron-works you may gather a cartload of it), *ergo* it is a martial herb." "The sun never shone upon a better herb for the yellow jaundice than this: why should men cry out so much upon Mars for an infortunate (or Saturn either)? Did God make creatures to do the creation a mischief? This herb testifies that Mars is willing to cure all diseases he causes; the truth is Mars loves no cowards, nor Saturn fools, nor I neither." "I would willingly teach astrologers, and make them physicians (if I knew how), for they are most fitting for the calling ; if you will not believe me, ask Dr. Hippocrates and Dr. Galen, a couple of gentlemen that our college of physicians keep to vapour with, not to follow. In this our herb, I shall give the pattern of a ruler, the sons of art rough cast, yet as near the truth as the men of Benjamin could throw a stone; whereby my brethren the astrologers may know by a penny how a shilling is coined : as for the college of physicians they are too stately to learn and too proud to continue. They say a mouse is under the dominion of the Moon, and that is the reason they feed in the night ; the house of the Moon is Cancer; rats are of the same nature as mice, but they are a little bigger; Mars receives his fall in Cancer, *ergo* Wormwood being an herb of Mars, is a present remedy for the biting of rats and mice."

"Wheals, pushes, black and blue spots, coming either by bruises or beatings, Wormwood, an herb of Mars, helps, because Mars (as bad as you love him, and as you hate him) will not break your head, but he will give you a plaister. If he do but teach you to know yourself, his courtesy is greater than his discourtesy." "Suppose a man be bitten or stung by a martial creature, imagine a wasp, a hornet, a scorpion, Wormwood, an herb of Mars, giveth you a present cure ; then Mars, choleric as he is, hath learned that patience, to pass by your evil speeches of him, and tells you by my pen, That he gives you no affliction, but he gives you a cure ; you need not run to Apollo, nor Æsculapius ; and if he were so choleric as you make him to be, he would have drawn his sword for anger, to see the ill-conditions of those people that can spy his vices, and not his virtues. The eternal God, when he made Mars, made him for public good, and the sons of men shall know it in the latter end of the world. *E cælum Mars solus habet.*"

There are two institutions for which old Culpepper cherished a bitter dislike—the College of Physicians and the Papacy. Wherever the smallest opportunity occurs he satirises one or the other. Referring to the Sea Wormwood and its various names, he says : " A Papist got the toy by the end, and he called it Holy Wormwood ; and in truth, I am of opinion, their giving so much holiness to herbs is the reason there remains so little in themselves." He also supposes that the Holy Thistle had its name "put upon it by some that had little holiness in themselves." When describing the virtues of the various species of Persicaria or Water-pepper, he tells us : " Our College of Physicians, out of the learned care of the publick good, *Anglice*, their own gain, mistake the one for the other in their 'New Master-piece,' whereby they discover—1. Their ignorance, 2. Their carelessness ; and he that hath but half an eye may see their pride without a pair of spectacles."

If a good handful of this plant (Persicaria) be put under a horse's saddle, it will make him travel faster, although he were half tired before.

But returning to Wormwood, he continues : "You say Mars is angry, and it is true enough he is angry with many countrymen for being such fools to be led

by the nose by the college of physicians, as they lead
bears to Paris garden. Melancholy men cannot bear
to be wronged in point of good fame, and that doth
sorely trouble old Saturn, because they call him the
greatest infortunate ; in the body of man he rules
the spleen (and that makes covetous men so sple-
netick), the poor old man lies crying out of his left
side. Father Saturn's angry, Mars comes to him ;
Come, brother, I confess thou art evil spoken of, and
so am I ; thou knowest I have my exaltation in thy
house, I give him an herb of mine, Wormwood, to
cure the poor man ; Saturn consented, but spoke
little, and so Mars cured him by sympathy." Then
we are treated to the account of some conversations
among the gods, with whom our author seems to have
been on the most familiar terms. He shows himself
superior to the opinions of men, for he winds up his
discourse on Wormwood thus :—

" He that reads this, and understands what he
reads, hath a jewel of more worth than a diamond ;
he that understands it not, is as little fit to give
physic. There lies a key in these words which will
unlock (if it be turned by a wise hand) the cabinet of
physic. I have delivered it as plain as I durst ; it is
not only upon Wormwood as I wrote, but upon all
plants, trees, and herbs ; he that understands it not,
is unfit (in my opinion) to give physic. This shall
live when I am dead. And thus I leave it to the
world, not caring a farthing whether they like or
dislike it. The grave equals all men, and therefore
shall equal me with all princes ; until which time the
eternal Providence is over me : Then the ill tongue

of a prating fellow, or one that hath more tongue
than wit, or more proud than honest, shall never
trouble me. *Wisdom is justified by her children.* And
so much for Wormwood."

The remark "I have delivered it as plain as I
durst" is evidently a little further indulgence in self-
exaltation, for on the last page he again remarks:
"You must not think, courteous people, that I can
spend time to give you examples of all diseases:
These are enough to let you see so much light as you
without art are able to receive: If I should set you
to look at the sun, I should dazzle your eyes, and
make you blind."

The leaves of the Common Alder-tree "gathered
while the morning dew is on them, and brought into
a chamber troubled with fleas, will gather them
thereunto, which, being suddenly cast out, will rid the
chamber of these troublesome bed-fellows."

The name Angelica affords him another opportunity
to rail against the physicians and Papists, and he
then gives the following directions for the gathering
of this plant:—"It is an herb of the Sun in Leo; let it
be gathered when he is there, the Moon applying to
his good aspect; let it be gathered either in his hour,
or in the hour of Jupiter, let Sol be angular; observe
the like in gathering the herbs of other planets, and
you may happen to do wonders." Very likely!

Anemone is "called also Wind-flower, because
they say the flower never opens save when the wind
bloweth. Pliny is my author; if it be not so, blame
him. The seed also (if it bears any at all) flies away
with the wind."

Garden Bazil "is the herb which all authors are together by the ears about, and rail at one another (like lawyers). Galen and Dioscorides hold it not fitting to be taken inwardly; and Chrysippus rails at it with downright Billingsgate rhetoric; Pliny and the Arabian physicians defend it." "Mizaldus affirms that, being laid to rot in horse-dung, it will breed venomous beasts. Hilarius, a French physician, affirms, upon his own knowledge, that an acquaintance of his, by common smelling to it, had a scorpion bred in his brain. Something is the matter, this herb and rue will not grow together, no, nor near one another; and we know rue is as great an enemy to poison as any that grows."

Bay-Tree. "It is a tree of the sun, and under the celestial sign Leo, and resisteth witchcraft very potently, as also all the evils old Saturn can do to the body of man, and they are not a few; for it is the speech of one, and I am mistaken if it were not Mizaldus, that neither witch nor devil, thunder or lightning, will hurt a man in the place where a Bay-tree is."

Of the Chamomile he remarks: "Nichessor saith, the Egyptians dedicated it to the sun, because it cured agues, and they were like enough to do it, for they were the arrantest apes in their religion I ever read of."

The Celandine is "called Chelidonium, from the Greek word Chelidon, which signifies a swallow, because they say, that if you put out the eyes of young swallows when they are in the nest, the old ones will recover their eyes again with this herb.

This I am confident, for I have tried it, that if we
mar the very apple of their eyes with a needle, she
will recover them again; but whether with this herb
or not I know not." After this confession of wanton
cruelty we will give but one more selection from this
barbarous old astrologer-herbalist. It refers to the
Devil's Bit Scabious :—

" This root was longer, until the Devil (as the
friars say) bit away the rest of it from spite, envying
its usefulness to mankind; for sure he was not
troubled with any disease for which it is proper."

CHAPTER XI.

ABOUT HORSETAILS, STONEWORTS, AND PEPPERWORTS.

THE non-botanical reader must not be deceived by the title of this paper. We do not intend to discourse

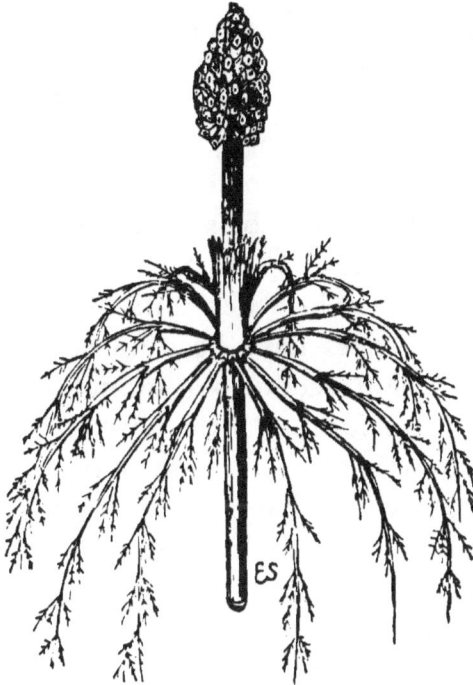

FIG. 115.

upon the hirsute appendages of the equine race, but upon a tribe of simple flowerless plants, scientifically known as the *Equisetaceæ*, a term which is almost literally translated in the popular name Horsetail.

They are leafless, many-jointed, hollow-stemmed plants, which spring from an underground rhizome. At the joints the stems are solid, and they fit together by a sort of sheath at the upper end of each joint, into which the lower end of the next joint fits. Immediately below the sheath a whorl of branches is given off, each branch being sheathed and jointed like the stem. A remarkable feature of this tribe of plants is the great quantity of silica, or flint, with which their stems are coated. In some this is so great that, on the plants being reduced to ashes, it is found that half the weight consists of silica. They may be macerated in water until the whole of the vegetable substances have been washed out, but the flinty coating still retains its form. This silica is deposited in the form of little crystals which give a rasp-like character to the stems; in fact, at least one species, *E. hyemale*, is largely used as a fine file for polishing wood, ivory, and metal. Large quantities are cultivated on the banks of the canals in Holland, and imported into this country under the name of Dutch Rush and Shave-grass. Their long, branching underground stems and interlacing roots tend to make the embankments more secure.

FIG. 116.

The fructification consists of a terminal cone, made up of stalked discs, which bear, on their under surface, a number of spore-cases, opening longitudinally. The spores are provided with four club-tipped elaters, which have peculiar hygrometric properties. If placed upon a glass-slide, breathed upon, and then placed under the microscope, these elaters will be seen to undergo some curious movements. " Some will be quite closed up, the elaters being so closely applied to the spores as to be scarcely distinguishable; others, again, will be seen gradually unfolding the filaments, and a few may be observed to move with a sudden start, as it were, from the contracted state of the elaters to that of full expansion. The ultimate cause of this movement is quite unknown. That it depends upon the amount of moisture with which the spores are surrounded there can be no doubt. Most probably it takes place by the contraction and expansion of the cells of which the elaters are composed, under the varying influence of the moisture contained in the air. The phenomenon is a very curious one, and should by all means be seen by every one who possesses a microscope" (H. W. S. in "Science Gossip," 1878).

FIG. 117.

FIG. 118.

FIG. 119.

The spore on germinating gives rise to a *prothallus* similar to that of ferns, and in the same manner bears *antheridia* and *archegonia*, which ultimately develop a true bud, and from this the new plant springs.

There are but ten British species, six of which are to be obtained in the London district. Some of them being very beautiful objects, might well be admitted to a place in the fernery, all that they require being plenty of moisture. The one thing to be sure of is, that the underground stem is obtained with its rootlets intact; it will then grow freely. Some of the species have the additional recommendation of being evergreen, though the deciduous kinds rival them in elegance.

The distribution of these remarkable plants is almost world-wide, some of the species attaining a considerable size; but they cannot approach the dimensions attained by representatives of the order in past ages. In the forests of the Carboniferous Period—when our coal was being formed—immense horsetails were abundant, reaching the height of thirty or forty feet, with a circumference of about fifteen inches! The remains of them have been found as fossils in the coal, and the name of *Calamites* applied to them.

" There is no doubt now that they are of the same family as our Equiseta, or Horsetails, a race which has, over most parts of the globe, dwindled down now from twenty or thirty feet in height, as they were in the old coal measures, to paltry little weeds. The tallest Equisetum in England—the beautiful *E. Telmateia*—is seldom five feet high. But they, too, are mostly mud and swamp plants, and so may the Calamites have been."—*Kingsley, " Town Geology."*

Somewhat resembling the Horsetails in appearance is a small tribe of delicate aquatic plants known as

the *Characeæ*, or Stoneworts. They have exceedingly
slender stems, but in spite of their slenderness and
brittleness they sometimes attain the length of three
or four feet. They are leafless, but, like *Equisetum*,
give off a whorl of branches from the nodes. The
plant is attached to the bottom of ponds and streams

FIG. 120.

FIG. 121.

by slender rootlets, which are also given off from the
nodes. The most remarkable feature of these plants
is the structure of the stem and branches. Each internode consists of a large and long cell (*axial cell*), invested by a number of spirally-arranged, smaller
and narrower cells (*cortical cells*), so transparent that
the axial cell can be seen through it. The axial cells
are separated at the nodes by a layer of smaller (*nodal
cells*), which is a continuation of the cortical layer.

The nodal cells give rise to the branches and whorled appendages, and to the organs of reproduction. Fig. 122 is a diagram of a longitudinal section through the plant, and will serve to show the relative size and position of these cells. A.C. shows the large axial cells, separated by N.C., the nodal cells, and invested by C.C., the cortical cells. Fig. 123 is a cross section in which A represents the axial cell, B the cortical cells.

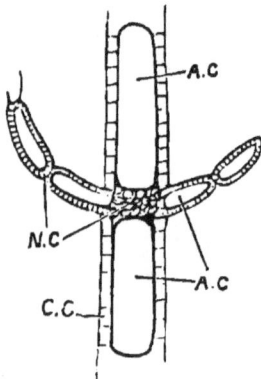

FIG. 122.

The most remarkable feature in *Chara* is what is known as its protoplasmic movements. If a portion of the plant be placed under the microscope, and a low-power objective used, these movements may be seen distinctly. If the focussing be adjusted so as to bring out the large axial cell, and observed carefully for a few seconds, the granules of protoplasm will be seen slowly, but uninterruptedly, to stream up one side of the cell and down the other. Similar movements in the protoplasm of cells may be seen in the American Pond-weed (*Anacharis alsinastrum*), *Vallisneria spiralis*, and in the hairs of Nettle and *Tradescantia*.

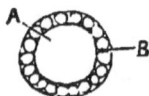

FIG. 123.

From the axils of the whorled appendages *Chara* produces two orange-coloured bodies—the *antheridia* and *sporangia*. The *sporangium* is an oval cell invested by five rows of spirally-twisted cortical cells, so arranged as to leave an aperture at the summit.

The *antheridium* is smaller and more globular in form, and consists of a cell-wall made up of eight pieces. From the inner surface of each of these pieces a short process called *manubrium* is developed (*m*, fig. 126), which bears on its summit (*capitulum*) six smaller processes (*secondary capitula*). These in turn give off each four long slender filaments (*f*, fig. 126), which are divided off into small cells. These cells in a single filament will number from one hundred to two hundred; and as there are nearly two hundred of these filaments in a single antheridium, the number of these cells will range from twenty to forty thousand in each antheridium. The protoplasm in the filament cells becomes ultimately developed into spirally-coiled tapering bodies, provided at the thin end with two delicate cilia. These are the antherozoids; and when the cells burst they are propelled along by the lashing of the cilia. The antherozoids enter the sporangium at its summit, and, it is believed, pierce the substance of the central cell, and fertilise it. The sporangium after a time drops off, falls into the mud, and germinates. A shoot is given off, which immediately divides, and sends a branch (its first root) down into the mud. The main shoot grows to a certain length, becomes divided into cells by transverse partitions, and ceases to grow.

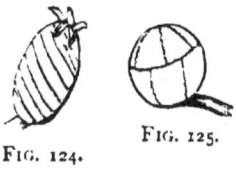

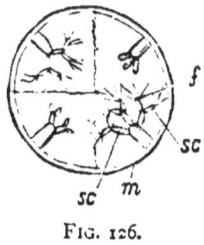

FIG. 124.

FIG. 125.

FIG. 126.

FIG. 127.

But from one of the cells a number of little processes are given off, and from the centre of these a bud, like

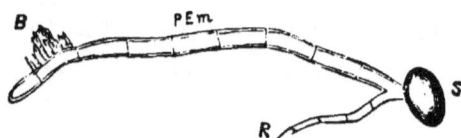

FIG. 128.

the growing point of an adult stem, arises, and gradually produces a new plant, with stem and branches, roots and reproductive organs complete. In fig. 128 S is the detached sporangia, which has given rise to the pro-embryo P.Em, with its root R, and bud B.

It should be noted that in *Chara* there are no vessels. The whole plant is built up of cells, each being originally of the simple form of cells, but some of them becoming ultimately modified. Thus the antherozoids are at first simple cells, becoming modified for a special purpose.

From the simple character of the organisation in these plants, the order occupies a low position in the classification of flowerless plants. Their place is between the Crystalworts (*Ricciaceæ*) and the Algæ.

It remains for us to notice the British representatives of an order called *Marsileaceæ*, or Pepperworts. There are but three British species, one of these— *Isoëtes Moorei*—having been discovered by Dr. Moore, as recently as 1879, in Upper Lake, Bray, co. Wicklow.

The English species are but two, each belonging to a different genus. They are both aquatic plants.

Isoëtes lacustris, the Quillwort, or Merlin's Grass, grows on the bottoms of lakes, being completely submerged, when it has the appearance of grass. The stem or root-stock is globular in form, and gives

off a number of erect, tapering leaves from four
to six inches in length.   These leaves consist of four
rows of long cells placed side by side, and subdivided
by transverse partitions.   It is these transverse partitions which show through the epidermis and give the
leaf the jointed appearance shown in fig. 129.   The

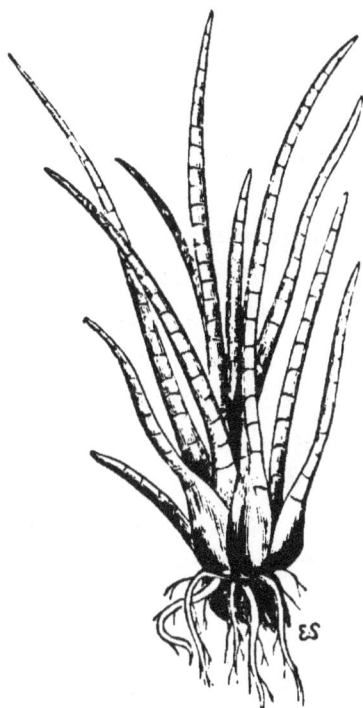

FIG. 129.

FIG. 130.

FIG. 131.

base of the leaf is very broad, and concave; within
the hollow it bears the fructification, which is of two
kinds.   The spore-cases produced by the outer leaves
contain large four-sided spores which open on the
upper surface by three triangular valves; whilst those
of the inner leaves are minute and more numerous.

These latter are evidently *antheridia*. The larger
spores germinate by division of the cells of the apex,
from which *archegonia* are formed. Fig. 130 represents a leaf with its spore-case, which is also shown
detached. Fig. 131 is a section of the spore-case
showing the three chambers into which it is divided.
The plant is rare in the south of England. The
name is derived from two Greek words, *Isos*, equal,
and *etos*, a year, in allusion to its leaves, which are
persistent during the whole year.

The remaining species is known as *Pilularia globu-
lifera*, the Pillwort, or Pepper-grass. It grows on
the margins of ponds and lakes,
and presents the appearance of
fig. 132. It has a creeping stem,
from which, at intervals, are given
off the fibrous roots which fix it
in the mud, and the small quill-
like leaves. These leaves are at
first rolled up in a circinate manner, like the fronds of ferns, and
vary in length from an inch to
four inches. They are hollow,
bright green, and smooth.

FIG. 132.

The spore-cases are attached by
a short stalk to the stem, at the
base of the leaves. They are
about the size of a pepper-corn,
from which fact the popular name has arisen ; they
are densely clothed with hairs, and, when ripe, split
open into four valves, to the centre of which the
spores and *antheridia* are attached. The lower part

of the spore-case is devoted to the large single spores; the upper produces the smaller, numerous granules, which ultimately yield spermatozoids, which fertilise the larger spores. This spore-case is represented at fig. 133.

Pilularia is more frequent in the south of Britain than *Isoëtes*, but it requires careful searching amongst the sedges to discover it. Both these plants are easily cultivated, *Isoëtes* forming a suitable object for the bottom of an aquarium. They belong, as we have stated, to the order *Marsileaceæ*, one species of which, *M. macropus*, affords

Fig. 133.

the fruit called Nardoo, which the Australian aborigines made up into a coarse kind of bread, and to which a melancholy interest attaches. When the exploring expedition of Messrs. Burke, Wills, and King had crossed the Australian continent from Melbourne to the Gulf of Carpentaria, they were reduced to sore straits on the return journey, finally perishing of starvation. This was their last resource, and Mr. King, who survived, brought some of the spores with him to Melbourne: there are specimens at Kew which were raised from these spores.

CHAPTER XII.

THE FALLING LEAF.

" Leaves have their time to fall,
And flowers to wither at the north wind's breath."
HEMANS.

EVERY one admires the beauties of the flower, but how few properly appreciate the glories of the foliage! Only at two short periods of the year do we usually deign to give them a word of admiration. In spring we all seem to sing the praises of Nature, as we behold the delicate fresh green tints of the bursting leaf-buds and the tiny leaflets. With them come the harbingers of summer, the bright flowers of spring, led off by the pure white of the

" Chaste Snowdrop, venturous harbinger of Spring,
And pensive monitor of fleeting years !"

followed by the ever-welcome

" Daisies, those pearled Arcturi of the earth,
The constellated flower that never sets,"

as Shelley sings ; perhaps the most-valued flower of all that blow, for though it cheers us by its presence nearly all the year, we yet esteem its innocent beauty when we are surrounded by all the floral wealth of

July and August.   Then come the pale cups of the
Wood Sorrel, and the wind-blown blooms of the

> "Delicate Anemone !
> Flower that seems not born to die
> With its radiant purity,
> But to melt in air away,
> Mingling with the soft spring day."

With these the pale sulphur of the Primrose and
the rich yellow of its meadow-loving relative the
Cowslip gradually lead on to the richer, warmer tints
of the advancing year, through the Buttercups, the
Violets, and Hyacinths.   With the flowers the leaves
also take on a warmer tint.   The light tender green
of the spring is toned down into the deeper tints of
summer.

Now we revel in a paradise of flowers—of every
conceivable form and hue, and a luxuriance of foliage
which we admire chiefly for the cool shade it affords.
But when autumn appears on the scene, and with a
touch turns the green leaves to the most glorious
shades of crimson, brown, and yellow, we give them
a different value, for the flowers are fading and we
miss their glowing colours.

> "With ev'ry gust the leaves pour down
>   And leave the bare unsightly stems ;
> Ah! what a little time has flown
>   Since those same leaves were budding gems.
> And now deft Nature's artist hand
>   Has softly toned their bright green down,—
> Their chlorophyll has slowly tanned
>   To rich warm hues of red and brown."

Then, when Nature sends her servants the winds
to whistle through the trees and strip the branches of

their leafy wealth, we begrudge her even this slight
return from the gifts she has bestowed so lavishly
upon us, forgetting that we shall get them all back
again a hundred-fold. For they but go back to her
laboratory to be re-manufactured into leaf-bud and
blossom, twig and branch again.

Here they come, racing and dancing, and flying on
the wings of the wind. Oh, what a rustle! strewing
the paths and fields and lanes with their dead bodies.
Dead?

> " And shall we say those leaves are dead,
> When naught in Nature ever *dies*?
> What though the plant its bloom has shed,
> It comes again in other guise!
> Last autumn's leaves, though buried low,
> Next spring will rise as leaf and flower,
> Though earth absorb the winter snow
> 'Twill come again as summer shower."

Surely not dead, for their mission is not completed.
And what, pray, is their mission? They are servants
of Madam Nature, who is *the* Lady Bountiful. In
her laboratory, which is the earth, she has a wonderful mill which we heard much of when we were
children—the mill which grinds old things into new.
All the beautiful gifts she bestows on man after a
while get shabby and the worse for wear, and then
man throws them from him and tramples them under
foot. Even these beautiful leaves which we call dead
we shall soon get tired of, and vote them a nuisance.
We shall sweep them up into a corner, and the wind,
again distributing them, we shall tread on them as
though they had never ministered to our pleasure.
But Nature will be on the look-out, and will set some

of her agents to work to bring them back again into her laboratory. It will take some months to do this, but she will not be idle in the meantime; she has always plenty of material in her magazines. She wants them first to protect the seeds and plants from that energetic servant of hers, the frost. Then they are attacked by various beetles and other insects, and gorgeous toadstools and other forms of fungi prey upon them; then the frost comes and helps, and between them all they break up the tissues and fibres, and even the very cells, of the leaf. And the rain and dew, and the melting snow, carry the particles slowly down into her stores ready for her use.

And from these remains she takes numbers of beautiful crystals of phosphate and oxalate of lime, and phosphoric and sulphuric acids; she also finds many other substances there which she carefully takes, and sends them through the tiny rootlets of the trees and plants into the big roots and up into the stems and branches. And here she forms them again into leaf-buds and flower-buds. And the wind and rain, the sun and dew, help them and bring them fresh substances again, and the buds expand into leaf and flower.

And so they go on, never stopping; for though in the cold, cheerless winter, when Nature herself seems gone to sleep, it is only apparently so, for she is still at work—hard at work in her workshops preparing the buds and blossoms for the coming spring. And then we see the value of these crystals from the dead leaves, in the beautiful silken flowers of the Crocus, the bright yellow blooms of the Cowslip and Primrose, the fronds of the ferns now unrolling, and vivid green new-born leaves expanding in myriads on every branch. And later in the year, when these green leaves are in their turn changed in hue, the value of these crystals will again be shown in the rosy apples and purple clusters of juicy grapes, and garners piled to the roof with golden grain.

Now that the leaves have fallen, let us take a ramble through the wood or on the heath, and though we shall enjoy our walk, our enjoyment is tinged with a feeling of sadness. We miss the beautiful foliage! There are the beautiful smooth-stemmed, giant beeches, fantastically gnarled and contorted, but their rich red autumn-tinted leaves are forming a thick crisp carpet below. The drooping branches of the silver-barked birch are naked. The clumps of furze are still enlivened by a few golden blooms, and the bracken is still glorious in its autumn tints. But there is a feeling of melancholy in the air. The beauty of the year has departed, and we think of approaching winter, with this heath and its bracken and furze and heather all covered by snow, and all its life stilled for a season.

> " Here still the daisy rears her head,
>   And buttercups still sparsely linger ;
> High in the heavens, with wings full spread,
>   Above us floats a glorious singer
> Whose song, though full of rapturous strains,
>   Seems to have caught a tone of sadness,
> As though he to the wind complains
>   For cutting short his summer gladness."

Yes! even the songs of the birds seem changed,

though that may be only the reflex of our own feelings. We know what we have lost for another five
months, and we therefore regret

> " The fall of Autumn,
> Its chilly evenings and its dropping leaves
> Bringing soft melancholy thoughts."

CHAPTER XIII.

ABOUT FUNGI.

FUNGI are an important class of flowerless plants, belonging to the division called *Thallogens*, those plants which have no distinction between stem and leaf. They consist wholly of cells, and are distinguished from other plants by the entire absence of chlorophyll (see Chapter II.) from their cells, which are also devoid of starch. Instead of absorbing carbon from the atmosphere, as do green plants, they absorb oxygen and give off carbon, in this respect resembling animals. Some of the lower forms were described in Chapter I.; we shall have occasion again to refer to several of these.

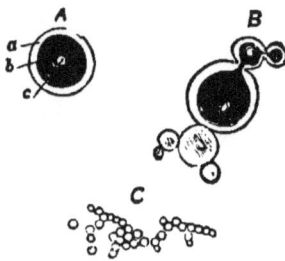

The Yeast-plant (*Torula*) we may take as a type of the fungus cell. Here, in fig. 134, we have enlarged representations of it. At A we have a single plant,— a simple cell, consisting of a cellulose wall (*a*) and a central mass of protoplasm (*b*), with a clear space or vacuole (*c*). In this it does not differ from ordinary vegetable cells, but its difference may be seen on

FIG. 134.

subjecting it to an experiment. Examined by the microscope, we note the absence of any green or red colouring matter. It has no chlorophyll. If we run in a little solution of iodine on the slide we shall observe that the protoplasm is stained brown; the cell-wall remains uncoloured. If starch were present it would be stained blue. *Torula*, therefore, has no starch, and this absence of starch is a characteristic of fungi.

If we place the slightest particle of yeast in a saccharine solution, we shall observe that the liquid, previously clear, has in a day or two become turbid. If we take up a small quantity of the liquid on the point of a pencil or a glass rod, and place it under the microscope, we shall find that the whole of the fluid is teeming with millions of *Torulæ*, which have been produced by the multiplication of the few we added to our liquid. We now take two bottles and half fill them with fresh saccharine fluid, then add the slightest drop of the turbid liquor to each, cork them both up, and place one in complete darkness, the other in the light. On examining them in a few days, we shall find that they are equally turbid. Therefore *Torula* is not dependent upon light for the power of growth; this also is a characteristic of fungi. On loosening the cork after a day or two, we shall notice a terrific rush of air or gas from the bottle, or if we fail to loosen or remove the cork the pressure from within will do it for us with considerable vehemence. But we can test this gas, and shall then find it to be carbonic anhydride, which is the same as the gas exhaled by animals. Here we have another characteristic of fungi, for we have seen (Chapter II. *ante*) that plants possessing chlorophyll give off oxygen.

Fungi are essentially either parasites or scavengers,—or both. We have seen (Chapter II.) that green plants have the power of constructing protein out of a few elementary substances. Not so fungi; their food must be *organised*,—that is, the elementary substances must be chemically combined to form a part of some previously existing animal or plant. Thus sugar is a vegetable product which consists of the chemical elements Carbon, Hydrogen, and Oxygen. Torula can grow and flourish in a solution of sugar and water, though it cannot live in a mixture of Carbon, Hydrogen, and Oxygen, unless they have been elaborated into a *compound* by being taken into the vegetable economy.

The reproduction of Torula is effected in the simplest manner possible. It either develops transverse partitions across the cell and thus divides itself into two or more cells; or, what is more common, it produces a swelling or bud at some point outside the cell-wall, and this bud grows into a full-sized cell identical in every respect with that from which it originated. Fig. 134, B, shows how this process of budding goes on.

All fungi are composed of cells similar in every respect to Torula, though in the higher species these cells are combined in a variety of ways to produce forms varying greatly from each other. As an advance in organisation upon Torula we have *Penicillium* (fig. 135). Here we have simply a number of cells like Torula, a little drawn out and placed end

to end. At its summit it bears a string of round
cells which, when separated from the plant, cannot
be distinguished from Torula. These are the spores
or *conidia*, which, if sown on an
appropriate substance, send out
shoots from various parts of the
cell-wall. These shoots are at first
simple elevations of the cell-wall,
like the budding of Torula, but
they continue to elongate by transverse division of the cells composing them until a considerable extent of surface is covered by their
ramifications. These shoots are
termed *hyphæ*, and the felt-like

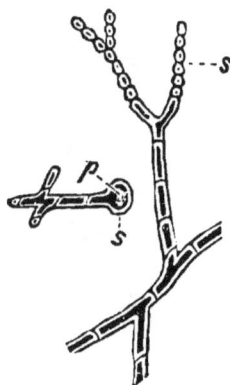

FIG. 135.

mass formed by their growth is known as the *mycelium*. These *hyphæ* send off branches above and
below; those above, which are erect, are the *aerial
hyphæ*, whilst those below are the *submerged hyphæ*,
and serve the purpose of roots. The *aerial hyphæ*
bear upon their summits the *conidia*, which also are
formed by the transverse division of the cells. It
should be noted that, neither in this nor in any other
form of fungus, do cells multiply by longitudinal
division.

Another form very similar to *Penicillium* is *Mucor*,
but in this the hypha consists of an undivided tube,
or a cell drawn out to a very great length. The
aerial hyphæ bear a large globular cell (the *sporangium*), which contains a large number of smaller cells
(*ascospores*). These ascospores are set free by the
bursting of the sporangium (or *ascus*, as we shall

have to call it hereafter), and, germinating, repeat the process described in *Penicillium*. But in this species there is an alternative method of reproduction shown in figs. 137 and 138. Two aerial hyphæ (H) in the same vicinity throw out a branch each. These branches have dilated ends which ulti- mately come into contact with each other. A septum or divi- sion is formed across the branch just below the dilated end, so that the branch becomes terminated by a cell. After these two cells come in contact, their applied faces become attached, the inter- vening cell-walls become absorbed, and the protoplasm of the two cells mingle and form one large cell—the *zygospore*. It is very different in

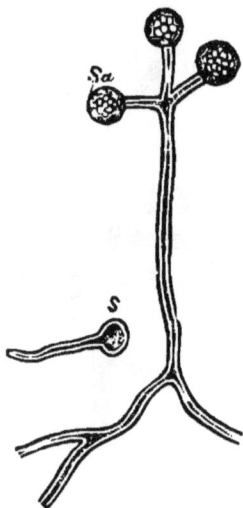

Fig. 136.

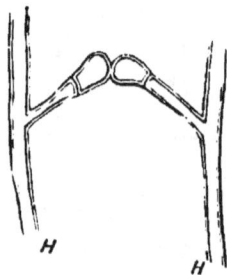

Fig. 137.

Fig. 138.

nature to the ascospore, for the latter, on germinating, gives rise directly to a perfect *Mucor;* but the zygo- spore produces a short hypha, which gives off an erect

prolongation, ultimately developed into a sporangium or ascus, containing many ascospores. This is
termed the "*alternation of generations*," and is similar
to the process of reproduction in ferns, previously
explained. A fern produces spores, one of which
germinating, gives rise, not to another fern—but to a
minute plant called a "prothallus," which bears antheridia and archegonia. The former fertilise the latter,
and as the result of such fertilisation a bud is formed
which develops into a perfect fern.

We have seen that these low forms of fungi increase
by cell-division, but only in one direction; the cells

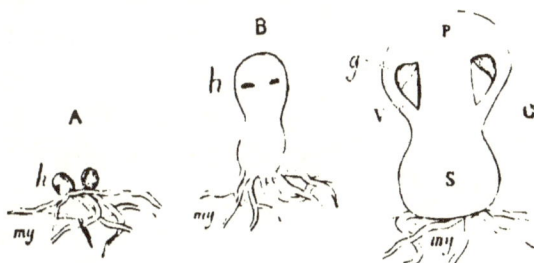

Fig. 139.

never divide laterally. This we shall find is a characteristic of all fungi, and we may see by examination of a mushroom or toadstool that the thickness
of their stems is attained by the growth of many
hyphæ side by side. Like Penicillium and Mucor
these larger plants arise from spores, which on
germinating give off hyphæ, branching and interlacing to form a *mycelium*. Fig. 139 illustrates the
development of an *Agaric* or Mushroom. A shows
the mycelium (*my*) with two little roundish protube-
rances (*h*), the future *hymenophore*. B is a section of

the *hymenophore* after it has attained considerable size, and C is a section of the same more highly developed ; *g* marks the embryo "gills" or plates which bear the spores; P is the future *pileus* or cap, joined to the stem (S) by a membrane (V), the *veil.* As the Mushroom grows this veil is broken, the stem elongates, the pileus expands, and the plant assumes its perfect shape. Fig. 140 represents a vertical section of a full-grown Agaric, in which A is the *annulus* or ring, the ruins of the veil. The other letters refer to the same parts as in fig. 139.

"A longitudinal slice from the stem will exhibit under the microscope delicate tubular cells, the general direction of which is lengthwise, with lateral branches, the whole interlacing so intimately that it is difficult to trace any individual thread very far in its course. It will be evident that the structure is less compact as it approaches the centre of the stem, which in many species is hollow. The *hyme-*

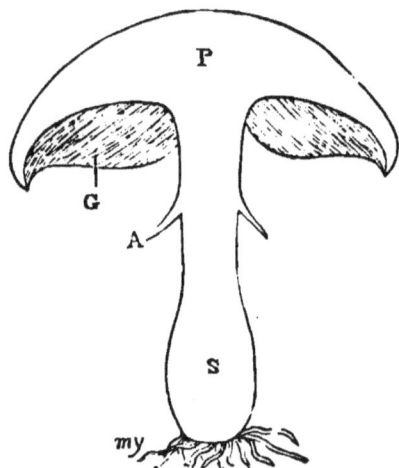

Fig. 140.

nium is the spore-bearing surface, which is exposed or naked, and spread over the gills. These plates are covered on all sides with a delicate membrane, upon which the reproductive organs are developed. If it were possible to remove this membrane in one entire piece, and spread it out flat, it would cover an immense surface, as compared with the size of the pileus, for it is plaited or folded like a lady's fan over the whole of the gill-plates, or lamellæ, of the fungus." *

It is upon the characters of the spore-bearing surfaces that the fungologist relies for guidance in classification. Upon these characters he classes all fungi in two great primary divisions, in the first of which (SPORIFERA) the spores are naked, *i.e.*, they are not enveloped in an *ascus;* in the second division (SPORIDIFERA) the spores *are* enclosed in *asci*, as in *Mucor*.

Fig. 141 shows the manner in which these spores are borne in Agarics. S is the spores which are borne in fours upon a projection (B, *the basidium*) from the gill-plate. On the variations in these spore-bearing organs the orders and genera are based; but it is impossible, in the limits of a chapter, to enter fully into the subject of classification, neither does such subject come within the scope of a popular book.

FIG. 141.

Those of our readers who wish to become fungologists we would refer to the works of the Rev. M. J. Berkeley, M.A., F.L.S., and Dr. M. C. Cooke, M.A.

Among this group of flowerless plants are to be found some of the most remarkable vegetable growths, and, without exaggeration, we may add, some of the most beautiful. No more delicately beautiful sight can be found among higher plants than a group of minute moulds under the microscope. It is a veri-

* Dr. M. C. Cooke.

table fairy forest, where the trees are of silver bearing pearls for fruit. And are not the larger forms also beautiful ? Visit the woods in autumn, and note the rich variety of form and colour exhibited by the larger species there.

"Of colour, fungi exhibit an almost endless variety, from white, through ochraceous, to all tints of brown until nearly black, or through sulphury yellow to reds of all shades, deepening into crimson, or passing by vinous tints into purplish black. These are the predominating gradations, but there are occasional blues and mineral greens, passing into olive, but no pure or chlorophyllous green. The nearest approach to the latter is found in the hymenium of some *Boleti*. Some of the Agarics exhibit bright colours, but the larger number of bright-coloured species occur in the genus *Peziza*. Nothing can be more elegant than the orange cups of *Peziza aurantia*, the glowing crimson of *Peziza coccinea*, the bright scarlet of *Peziza rutilans*, the snowy whiteness of *Peziza nivea*, the delicate yellow of *Peziza theleboloides*, or the velvety-brown of *Peziza repunda*. Amongst Agarics, the most noble *Agaricus muscarius*, with its warty crimson pileus, is scarcely eclipsed by the Continental orange *Agaricus cæsarius*. The amethystine variety of *Agaricus laccatus* is so common and yet so attractive ; whilst some forms and species of *Russula* are gems of brilliant colouring. The golden tufts of more than one species of *Clavaria* are exceedingly attractive, and the delicate pink of immature *Lycogala epidendrum* is sure to command admiration. The minute forms which require the microscope, as much to exhibit their colour as their structure, are not wanting in rich and delicate tints, so that the colour-student would find much to charm him, and good practice for his pencil in these much despised examples of low life" (Cooke).

But the reader may fancy it is not enjoyable work hunting for fungi in autumn when the woods are damp. Hear what Mr. Worthington G. Smith, F.L.S., has to say upon that point: " The study of the larger fungi has been to me one of the greatest pleasures of my life: when all things else have failed, this has never failed; it has taken me into the pleasantest of places and amongst the best of people. Had it not been for fungi, I should have been dead years ago; often tired, jaded, and harassed with business matters, a stroll in the rich autumn woods has given me a new lease of life. In these favourite haunts I never tire or flag; rain, fog, and mud never detract from the pleasure of the woods to me,—I am only depressed in the hot, dry weather of midsummer. In the autumn I constantly visit the forests, with all my collecting paraphernalia; I sometimes take a saw to cut off the big, woody, fungous excrescences of trees. I was once fortunate enough to find a ladder in a wood, which proved invaluable for ascending the beeches in search of *Agaricus mucidus*, &c. I, however, find fungi everywhere: I only go round the corner, and there they are. I often visit a neighbouring builder's yard, and descend the sawpits, to the amazement of the operatives: some of the rarest species of our flora, and many new ones, I have found within a few minutes' walk of my own house. I once found a rare *Lentinus* on a log as it was being

carted down King William Street, and a year or
so ago an undescribed *Peziza* flourished inside my
cistern."

Besides the pleasure of healthy association with
beautiful scenery obtained in searching for them,

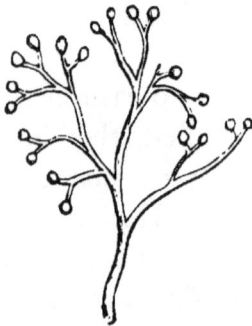

FIG. 142.

fungi have a claim upon our attention for other reasons. First,
they are by no means insignificant factors in the economy of
Nature. As we have said, they
are parasites and scavengers.
Much of the natural food of man
is destroyed by these plants, and
for this reason alone we ought
to know something about them.
One of the most troublesome
fungi in this respect is *Peronospora infestans*, the
Potato fungus, to which we have referred at some

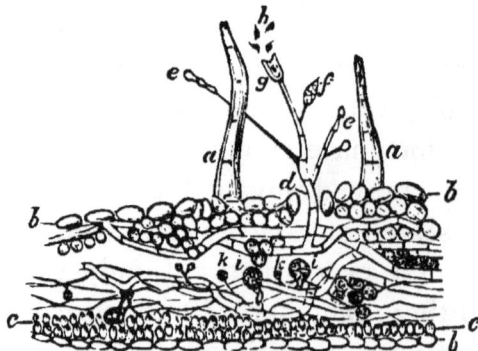

FIG. 143.

length in Chapter I. As will be seen, on reference
to fig. 142, it is one of the moulds, somewhat resembling Mucor. Fig. 143 shows a section of the potato

leaf, with the *Peronospora* mycelium ramifying among, and attacking, its cells. *Peronospora gangliformis* attacks lettuces; *P. effusa* is found on spinach; *P. Schleideniana* is very destructive to young onions, and *P. trifoliorum* attacks the lucerne crops. So that here we have five species of one family preying upon and destroying man's food. *Puccinia graminis* causes the "rust" so destructive to wheat, and *P. apii* attacks the leaves of celery. We have elsewhere alluded to the evident polymorphism of this species and its connection with *Æcidium* (fig. 144). *Cystopus candidus* and *Glæsporium concentricum* are destructive to the cabbage tribe; *Trichobasis fabæ* fatal to the growth of beans. The pear is attacked by *Ræstelia*

FIG. 144.

cancellata; the plum by *Puccinia prunorum*, and other fruit trees suffer under the growth of various species.

Oidium (fig. 145) is the well-known Vine disease, and fig. 146 represents *Erysiphe*, the pea-blight. Many of our garden flowers are attacked by various species, among them roses, which suffer from at least four different species. Violets, anemones, orchids, hollyhocks, pelargoniums, sweet-williams, and ferns are among the victims of fungi in our gardens. A few years ago serious fears were entertained by horticulturists lest

FIG. 145.

the whole race of hollyhocks should be destroyed by the ravages of *Puccinia malvaccarum*, a species

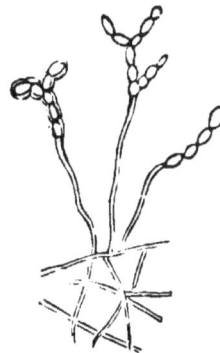

which has found its way here from South America. Timber trees, too, suffer terribly from fungi, among the most destructive being several species which are known under the general term of "dry rot;" the state of wood so attacked is well known, though it is perhaps not quite so well known how it is caused. One of the most destructive of these species is *Merulius lacrymans*, which Fig. 146. penetrates the cells of the wood, and robs them of their lignine and cellulose, thus rendering their tissue friable.

The effects of fungi upon animals is no less remarkable. Many insects are attacked by fungi during life. *Botrytis Bassiana* is a great impediment to the production of silk owing to its destruction of the silkworm. It is known under the popular name of Muscardine. The spores are probably eaten by the silk-worm, as they seem to commence growth in the insect's large intestine; though if the spores be simply rubbed upon the silkworm's skin, they will germinate, and their threads prey upon the fatty tissue till the whole of the insect's body be filled with them. Most of our readers must have noticed how in autumn the flies stick to the window-panes after death, though their extended limbs and fresh appearance might lead one to suppose they were still alive. On closer examination we shall find that the fly is standing upon a mat of delicate silk threads spread upon the glass. These threads are really the mycelium of a fungus which attacks the fly. The fly becomes sluggish, and rests upon some surface, preferably on the window-pane, and passively awaits the triumph of its enemy. This fungus was formerly known under the name of *Empusa muscæ*, though it is now known to be only a terrestrial condition of a species of *Saprolegnia*, the fungi which attack fish, covering them with a coat of white threads.

But if fungi are enemies of insects, insects retaliate by making food of fungi. Many beetles are altogether dependent upon fungi in this respect, and the Coleopterist knows that large numbers of them may be obtained by simply breaking open or shaking various fungi. Man, too, who suffers greatly, as we have seen, from the effects of fungi, gets some good from them by using them as food. But we may safely say that comparatively little of the abundant supply of wholesome species of fungi is used for food. With the exception of a few well-known species, which are sold under the general title of mushrooms and truffles, the public are afraid of them. Nor is this fear without foundation, for, as is well known, many species are deadly poisonous in their effects upon the human system when taken as food. But there is no doubt that prejudice has more to do with the matter than fear, for if prejudice were absent mankind would have found out long ago which species were to be avoided and which eaten. As it is, the harvest of the woods and pastures is gathered only by the privileged few —the fungologists, who can distinguish the species. These authorities give us particulars as to the flavour and tenderness of the several species that must make the mouth of the tyro water. Dr. Badham, our highest authority upon edible fungi, says :—

" I have this autumn myself witnessed whole

hundredweights of rich wholesome diet rotting under trees; woods teeming with food, and not one hand to gather it; and this perhaps in the midst of potato-blight, poverty, and all manner of privations, and public prayers against imminent famine. I have indeed grieved, when I consider the straitened condition of the lower orders, this year to see pounds innumerable of extempore beefsteaks growing on our oaks in the shape of *Fistulina hepatica; Agaricus fusipes*, to pickle, in clusters under them; Puff-balls, which some of our friends have not inaptly compared to sweetbread, for the rich delicacy of their unassisted flavour; *Hydna*, as good as oysters, which they somewhat resemble in taste; *Agaricus deliciosus*, reminding us of tender lamb-kidney; the beautiful yellow Chantarelle, growing by the bushel, and no basket but our own to pick up a few specimens on our way; the sweet nutty *Boletus*, in vain calling himself *edulis*, when there was none to believe him; the dainty Orcella, the *Agaricus heterophyllus*, which tastes like the crawfish, when grilled; the red and green species of Agaricus, cooked in any way, and equally good in all."

Here is an opening for the epicure, here is a chance for the badly fed! Is not that paragraph sufficient justification for the labours and studies of fungologists? Tons of food wasted yearly through ignorance, whilst hundreds of people are starving in our midst. Would it not be a good thing if, in our Training Colleges, our future schoolmasters were taught to discriminate between the good and the noxious fungi, that those who received appointments to country schools might instruct the village children on the subject? Mr. Worthington G. Smith has published, in two sheets, coloured figures of the most common edible and poisonous fungi, which deserve a place upon the walls of every village school and club.

With reference to the habitats of fungi—they are truly ubiquitous. "We need not travel from home for examples: the unwelcome dry-rot may have committed its ravages beneath our kitchen floor, or the walls of our cellars, and our casks or bottles of wine may be infected with numbers of this ubiquitous race. Can we find no morsel of bread or cheese upon which a mould is flourishing? No towel or other article of household linen presenting traces of mildew? Are we perfectly certain that all our preserves are unvisited? or, to come nearer to some of us, all our books untouched? But in places which many would consider more unlikely still, we may look for and expect to find fungi: on whitewashed walls, plaster ceilings, dirty glass, old flannel, and old boots and shoes, or leather of any description; on carpets, mats, and boards; and even the plants of our herbaria must be watched against their ravages. Animals bear them about on their horns and hoofs, and the housefly often carries on its body the vegetating fungus, which ultimately deprives it of life. The yeast that is employed in fermenting our bread and our beer is a fungus, as well as the mildew and smut that infest our growing corn. From cesspools and traps the minute dust-like spores of hidden fungi rise into our dwellings; unseen they float in the air, entering everywhere, depositing themselves everywhere, and vegetating wherever the conditions are favourable to their development" (Cooke).

Mr. Worthington Smith tells us: "It is hardly necessary to specify localities, because fungi abound everywhere. If leaf fungi are sought for, hedge-sides will produce an abundant crop; if the Agaricini and Polyporei, forests and woods must be ransacked; if the edible species are wanted, rich open pastures (with few exceptions) must be traversed: the various species of truffles must be looked for principally in leafy glades—many prefer a calcareous subsoil, but at times they may be met with even in hedge-sides, town parks, or elsewhere."

When collected they should be placed in a current of *dry* air for some hours (six to twelve or twenty-four, according to size and degree of hardness), so that all superfluous moisture may be got rid of. If the weather be dry such a current may be obtained by raising the window-sash an inch or two, and placing the fungi close to it. They must then be treated in the same manner as ferns and flowering-plants,—gently pressed between sheets of drying paper until they are ready to be placed in the herbarium. But the collector should be careful not to leave his harvest in any damp atmosphere for a night, for in all probability he would next morning find that many of them had actually melted away, leaving only a dirty patch and a few black shreds to mark where they had been.

But our space is getting exhausted; there is much we might add to what we have written, but our object has been merely to give a slight general indication of the wonders that are to be found by the student of botany. Full information respecting any particular group of plants here mentioned must be sought for in the works of the authorities we have quoted.

It may not be out of place to conclude this chapter with another extract from Mr. W. G. Smith. He says :—

"Collecting fungi is not without its humours as well as its pleasures, as the following will show. I once saw a portly, well-dressed gentleman walking along the high-road, with his vasculum over his shoulders, and carrying home (one in each hand) a pair of cast-off, rotten boots, discarded by some vagrant ; the rotting leather having produced a crop of rare microscopic fungi. At times abominable cast-off fœtid gipsy rags will be lovingly taken from out a ditch, and choice pieces cut out and consigned to the vasculum of the crypto-gamic botanist ; at other times some rare species will be seen 'up a tree,' and it has several times happened in my presence that one enthusiastic botanist has got on to the shoulders of another to secure a prize, or even waded into a pond to get at some prostrate fungus-bearing log. The humours of truffle-hunting are manifold. I have seen a gentleman trespass, on hands and knees, through a holly-hedge, on to a gentle-man's lawn, and there dig up the turf in some promis-ing spot, risking an attack from the house-dog, or a few shots from the proprietor ; the said trespasser meanwhile armed with a rake, gouge, and dangerous-looking open knife. Country labourers are often sorely puzzled by the acts of cryptogamic botanists ;

they stand agape in utter amazement to witness poisonous 'frog-stools' bagged by the score. Oft-times one gets warned that the plants are 'deadly pisin;' but collectors are generally looked upon as harmless lunatics, a climax in this direction generally being reached if a gentleman, in search of *Ascoboli* and the dung-borne Pezizæ, sits down, and after making a promising collection of horse or cow dung, carefully wraps up these treasures in tissue paper, and puts them in his 'sandwich-box.'"

FIG. 147.—*Cyathus vernicosus*, or Bird's-nest Fungus.

CHAPTER XIV.

ALGÆ.

THE *Algæ* form an important order of cryptogamic
plants, comprising, however, the very simplest of all
plants. It includes at once some of the smallest and
some of the largest of plants, among the former being
many of the interesting microscopic organisms referred to briefly in Chapter I. Most of them are
marine or freshwater plants, only a few species being
found on land. All the seaweeds of our coasts, with
their lovely tints and beautiful forms, are *Algæ*. They
are characterised by the entire absence of *true* roots.
Many of them are attached to the rocks by pseudo-
roots; but attachment seems to be the only advantage obtained by this arrangement. Instead of being
dependent upon these pseudo-roots for nourishment,
they absorb it through every part of their surface.
They are entirely cellular in their structure, though
a few possess organs closely approaching to vessels.
In outward form they exhibit a remarkable amount
of variation, many of the higher forms being possessed of thick, solid stems, like tree-trunks, as in
Lessonia, which forms submarine forests. In the
opposite direction, we have such forms as *Protococcus*,
Desmid, and *Volvox*, which consist of a single cell

each, and consequently have neither stem, leaf, nor root.

We have elsewhere seen that *Protococcus* absorbs carbon, and sets free oxygen. In this respect all the Algæ agree, and to this power the denizens of the deep, in all their marvellous variety and infinite number, owe their existence. It is frequently stated that the ocean owes its power of sustaining life to its ceaseless motion keeping it constantly oxygenated.

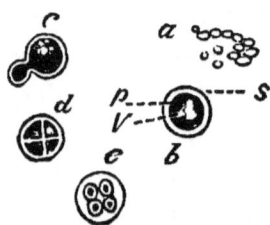

FIG. 148.

But the animal population of the deep is so enormous, and the consequent consumption of oxygen so vast, that this process alone would be insufficient to keep such an immense body of water pure. The submarine forests, which consist entirely of *Algæ*, give off an immense volume of oxygen, besides supplying the finny tribes, the crustaceans, and the molluscs, with the staple of their food.

There are several methods by which *Algæ* are reproduced. In the lower forms reproduction takes place by the repeated subdivision of an individual plant. In others it is attained by two individuals throwing out little processes, which come in contact, unite, and form a spore. In the higher forms the reproductive process is correspondingly more complicated.

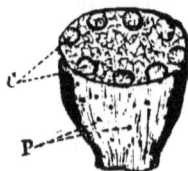

FIG. 149.—Section of *Fucus ves culosus.*

In these two kinds of bodies are formed—the Sporangia and Antheridia. Fig. 149 shows a cross section of the stem of a species of

Fucus. C shows the position of the Conceptacles, which contain Sporangia, and P denotes the pores or openings of the Conceptacles. In fig. 150 one of these conceptacles is enlarged.
O is the external orifice (P in fig. 149), P the *perispores* or sporangia. In some species the Antheridia are contained within the same conceptacle as the perispores; in others they are contained in separate concep-

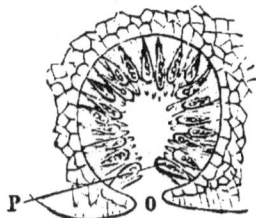

FIG. 150.—*Conceptacle.*

tacles on the same or other plants. They consist of ovoid sacs containing two *Spermatozoids* with cilia. When set free they enter the conceptacle by its external orifice or pore, attach themselves to a *perispore*, penetrate one of the spores contained therein, and by thus mingling their protoplasms, fertilisation of the spore is effected.

Algologists divide this group of plants into five subdivisions, as follows:—

1. Olive-coloured seaweeds (*Melanospermeæ*).
2. Rose-coloured seaweeds (*Rhodospermeæ*).
3. Green-coloured seaweeds (*Chlorospermeæ*).
4. Brittleworts (*Diatomaceæ*).
5. Volvoces (*Volvocineæ*).

The first of these (*Melanospermeæ*) comprises the various species of *Fucus* and *Laminaria* so plentiful on all our coasts. Every visitor to the seaside must be familiar with several species of *Fucus*, long lines of which are left by the receding tide. Who has not turned over quantities of this leathery jetsam to find the tiny crabs which seek shelter beneath it, with a motley collection of star-fishes, sea-urchins, mussels, and the remarkable clusters of eggs of the whelk and cuttlefishes? Here, too, it is we find those strange eggs of the dog-fish—Mermaids' purses as they are popularly called, as though such superior beings as the Mer-folk would be troubled with such things as purses! We do not believe they are possessed of pockets wherein to keep them if they had them.

But you recollect the seaweeds? First of all there is that tough, brownish species with narrow-branching fronds studded here and there—chiefly where the frond branches out—with air-bladders, which children are fond of exploding by pressure between finger and thumb. This is the Bladder Wrack or *Fucus vesiculosus,* and is most common on all rocky shores, covering as it does great areas of low rocks along the shore. We have painful recollections of this species. Not infrequently have we, in hurrying over the wrack-covered rocks, elated with some choice find, slipped on the fronds of this plant and been hurled flat on our back on the rugged, uneven surface of the rocks. The office of the bladders is, of course, to give buoyancy to the

FIG. 151.—*Fucus nodosus,* Knotted Fucus.

plant. In an allied species, *Fucus nodosus* or Knotted Wrack, of which we give an illustration (fig. 151), the bladders look as though strung on a line. This species attains the length of six feet. In *Halidrys siliquosa* the bladders very strongly resemble the seed-pods of the furze. To this group also belong the long, broad, olive fronds with crisped edges so frequently brought from the seaside to act as an indicator of the amount of moisture in the atmosphere. Its name is *Laminaria saccharina*, and, like its allies, *L. digitata* and *L. bulbosa*, it grows to an immense size. These plants annually lose the outer coating or *lamina* of their fronds, which falls off, revealing a new frond which has been formed within. They are most plentiful in the north. Another species resembles a gigantic leather bootlace, from twenty to forty feet in length. This is the *Chorda filum*, or Sea-lace. The frond is hollow and slimy, and when growing in the quiet waters of land-locked bays, attains its greatest dimensions. In the Carrêg Roads, off Falmouth, we have seen great areas of water occupied by this species, which sometimes obstructs to some extent the passage of boats. It is said seriously to endanger the life of the unfortunate swimmer who happens to pass through a bed of these tenacious laces, by clinging to his limbs and entangling him in a network from which there is no escape. In the genus *Lessonia* the species form submarine forests, the stems attaining the diameter of a couple of feet. The dead stems when thrown ashore are often mistaken for driftwood. They are said to be used with great success as the handles for knives and forks; the blade being pressed in while the stem is fresh and soft, is securely fixed by contraction of the latter in drying. But probably the most remarkable genus of these dark-spored *Algæ* is *Macrocystis*.

"From a much-branched root springs, in the first instance, a small forked frond which alone bears the fruit in clouded patches. . . . Besides this, however, arise one or more tall, slender stems, several feet in length, with a vertical, terminal, lanceolate frond, which is repeatedly split from the base upwards in such a way as to form new leaves, the attenuated base of which gradually passes into a short petiole, which becomes inflated above into a bladder. The original frond is thus repeatedly divided in a secund manner, till the plant becomes hundreds of feet long. As, however, the stem does not increase in strength as the plant elongates, the strain is at length so great, notwithstanding the numerous bladders, that it at last gives way, and the plant floats. Many species have been proposed by authors, but all are reducible to one, *M. pyrifera*, which girds the southern temperate zone, and stretches up from thence along the Pacific to the Arctic regions, through 120 degrees of latitude. This plant, like the *Sargassum*, has been celebrated by all voyagers, to whom it is of great value in indicating the presence of rocks, acting, as it does, like a great buoy. Vast masses are thrown up on exposed coasts, where it is rolled by the waves till it forms cables as thick as a man's body. Single plants have been estimated on reasonable grounds as attaining a length of 700 feet."—*Berkeley*.

Mr. Darwin, in his "Voyage of the Beagle," gives

us some account of the same plant as he encountered
it off Tierra del Fuego. He says it "grows on every
rock, from low-water mark to a great depth, both on
the outer coast and within the channels. I believe
during the voyages of the 'Adventure' and 'Beagle,'
not one rock near the surface was discovered which
was not buoyed by this floating weed. The good
service it thus affords to vessels navigating near
this stormy land is evident; and it certainly has
saved many a one from being wrecked. I know
few things more surprising than to see this plant
growing and flourishing amidst those great breakers
of the western ocean, which no mass of rock, let it
be ever so hard, can long resist. The stem is round,
slimy, and smooth, and seldom has a diameter of so
much as an inch. A few taken together are sufficiently
strong to support the weight of the large loose stones,
to which, in the inland channels, they grow attached;
and yet some of these stones were so heavy that,
when drawn to the surface, they could scarcely be
lifted into a boat by one person. . . . The beds of
this seaweed, even when not of great breadth, make
excellent natural floating breakwaters. It is quite
curious to see, in an exposed harbour, how soon the
waves from the open sea, as they travel through the
struggling stems, sink in height, and pass into smooth
water." And a little further on in his interesting
narrative, he says: "I can only compare these great
aquatic forests of the southern hemisphere, with the
terrestrial ones in the intertropical regions."

The only other example of the *Melanospermeæ* we
are able to find room for is the beautiful Peacock's

Tail, or Turkey-feather Laver of our southern shores (*Padina pavonia*), fig. 152. The fronds, which are marked with concentric lines, assume more or less the form of a cup. It is most common in tropical countries, and in our country only to be found on the most southern coasts.

FIG. 152.—*Padina pavonia.*

As a sample of the *Rhodospermeæ* we could desire no more lovely example than the Scarlet Plocamium (*Plocamium coccineum*), fig. 153, which is admired by all visitors to the seaside. The frond, which is of a beautiful rosy hue, is much divided, and has a delicate feathery appearance. Another well-known species of this group is the *Chondrus crispus*, better known by its popular title of Carrageen or Irish Moss. It is one of the commonest species on all our coasts, and may often be found washed up on the beach.

FIG 153 —*Plocamium coccineum.*

Its general form may be seen in the illustration (fig. 154), and in colour it varies from white, through yellow and greenish, up to a dull purple. It contains a large amount of gelatine, and when boiled produces a nutritious jelly, which is often prescribed for consumptives, for which purpose it is said to be far more valuable than ordinary animal gelatine. Another of the Rhodosperms used for food is the Dulse or Dillusk of the Scotch. Botanically it is the *Rhodymenia palmata*. In texture it is very tough, but yet not to be despised by the hungry, by whom it is eaten raw. Frequently sold with it under the

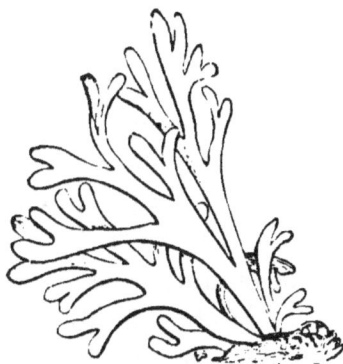

FIG. 154.—*Chondrus crispus.*

same name are the tough, dark-red fronds of *Iridæa edulis.*

Of the third division, the *Chlorospermeæ,* we have a familiar marine example in the *Ulva latissima* or Sea-lettuce, which consists of a very thin flat green frond (fig. 155). It is sometimes known as the Green Laver, on account of its being eaten like the true Laver (*Porphyra vulgaris*), which is by some esteemed a great luxury, and perhaps by as many regarded with

FIG. 155.—*Ulva latissima.*

disgust. Another species (*U. lactuca*) is frequently attached to oysters, and hence termed Oyster Green. In Scotland it is sometimes used as a remedy for headache by being bound round the temples.

In this group also occur the *Confervæ*—the Yoke-threads—*Oscillatoriæ*, and *Protococci*, described in our first chapter, to which we refer our readers.

Formerly these seaweeds yielded a rich harvest to the proprietors of coast-lands. They were collected in immense quantities, piled on the shore and burned, the result being a solid cake of ash. This ash was known as "Kelp," and consisted largely of carbonate of soda and salts of potash, which are largely used in the manufacture of soap. This "kelp" formed a source of considerable revenue to those who possessed lands on the coast, by the sale of it to the soap manufacturers. But modern researches in chemistry have shown that carbonate of soda can be more cheaply obtained from common salt, and so the kelp industry has dwindled to very small proportions, and the chief use to which the "harvest of the sea" is now put is in the manufacture of manure. But there is also another and a most important use to which seaweeds are put—that is, in the production of a valuable substance called *Iodine*. The discovery was made in the early part of this century by a soap-maker of Marseilles, named Courtois, who noticed a blue vapour arising from his vats during the rapid evaporation of the ley. This circumstance led to the discovery of iodine, which is now such an important substance in medicine and the arts.

Certain species of seaweeds are also employed to feed sheep and cattle. But probably the greatest value of this class of plants consists in the fact that they form at once the home and the food of countless species of fish, molluscs, and crustaceans; and, further, without their presence and oxygenating effects the ocean would be uninhabitable. No living thing could exist within its bounds, and, instead of being the highway of the world's commerce, it would become unnavigable—in fact, it would be one gigantic cess-pool, the receptacle of the world's sewage. Instead of the breezes from its bosom bringing the health-giving iodine and ozone to mankind, it would poison the whole atmosphere with its fœtid emanations; and all along the coasts there would be desolation and death for miles. Think, then, of the importance of this tribe of plants, lowly as are their position in the botanists' classification. Even the minute confervæ and diatoms of our ponds and streams are of the utmost importance in purifying the waters and sustaining the great numbers of animals that subsist upon decaying substances. Though the lowliest of all forms of life, they are, nevertheless, indispensable to the higher forms; and for this reason alone they merit some attention from us who stand at the other end of the scale of organisation.

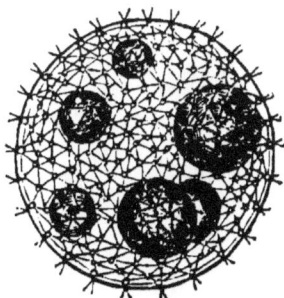

Fig. 156.—*Volvox globator.*

APPENDIX.

—o—

A TABLE OF THE *CRYPTOGAMIA*, OR FLOWERLESS PLANTS.

It may be objected that in the foregoing pages there is no systematic treatment of the various groups of flowerless plants. This is intentional. We have briefly alluded to all the orders of cryptogams, but have entirely ignored the position of these orders in scientific classification. For instance, we have grouped together what are popularly known under the general term of Mosses, although some are widely separated from the others in classification. Our reason for doing so is the fact that this book is intended for the non-scientific reader. For the benefit of those who wish to ascertain the proper relation of these orders to each other, we append a table of the classification of these plants.

SUB-KINGDOM III.—*Cryptogamia.*

Plants propagated by spores, having no embryo. Stems (when present) growing from the summit only. Leaves (when present) with forked venation. Bearing no true flowers.

    SUB-CLASS I.—*Acrogenæ.*

    SUB-CLASS II.—*Thallogenæ.*

Acrogenæ.

Vascular plants possessing distinct stem and leaves (or *fronds*). With stomata.

> ORDER   I.—*Filices,* or Ferns.
> ,,   II.—*Equisetaceæ,* or Horsetails.
> ,,   III.—*Marcileaceæ,* or Pepperworts.
> ,,   IV.—*Lycopodiaceæ,* or Club-mosses.
> ,,   V.—*Musci,* or True Mosses.
> ,,   VI.—*Jungermanniaceæ,* or Scale-mosses.
> ,,   VII.—*Marchantiaceæ,* or Liverworts.
> ,, VIII.—*Ricciaceæ,* or Crystalworts.
> ,,   IX.—*Characeæ,* or Stoneworts.

Thallogenæ.

Cellular plants, with no distinction between stem and leaf. No stomata.

> ORDER I.—*Lichenes,* Lichens.
> ,,   II.—*Fungi,* Mushrooms and Moulds.
> ,,   III.—*Algæ,** Seaweeds.

* Besides the Seaweeds and Confervæ, this order comprises the *Diatoms, Desmids,* and *Volvoces* described in Chapter I.

INDEX.

— o —

PRINTED BY BALLANTYNE, HANSON AND CO
LONDON AND EDINBURGH

MARSHALL JAPP & Co.'s

BOOK LIST.

17, HOLBORN VIADUCT,

LONDON, E.C.

January, 1881.

Messrs. MARSHALL JAPP & COMPANY'S

NEW BOOKS.

LABOUR AND VICTORY: Memoirs of those
who deserved success and won it.

Crown 8vo.   Cloth extra, with portraits, 3s. 6d.

Sir James Outram.	Sir William Ellis, the
Bishop Selwyn.	South-Sea Missionary.
Thomas Edward.	Sir James Simpson.
Thomas Davidson, the	Sir Titus Salt.
Scottish Probationer.	Friedrich Augusti.

WISE WORDS AND LOVING DEEDS: A
Book of Biographies for Girls.   By E. CONDER GRAY.
Crown 8vo.   Cloth extra, with portraits, 4s. 6d.

CONTENTS.

Mary Somerville.	Madame Feller.
Lady Duff Gordon.	Baroness Bunsen.
Sarah Martin.	Amelia Sieveking.
Ann Taylor.	Mary Carpenter.
Charlotte Elliott	Catherine Tait.

OPINIONS OF THE PRESS.

" A series of brightly-written sketches of lives of remarkable women.   The subjects are well chosen and well treated."—*Saturday Review.*

" We have much pleasure in commending to notice this series of admirable concise biographies of those, whose examples in different spheres of usefulness are so well adapted to stir up others to carry on the labours to which they devoted time and energy, and in still more instances to bring to the performance of everyday duties the same true-hearted devotion and earnest self-sacrifice."—*Nonconformist.*

" Told in a simple and pure style, very free from that inclination to point a moral in season and out of season, still more from the sickly piety which are the faults of most books written for the young. It opens with an account of the life of Mary Somerville, than which no more appropriate example could be set before girls.   The life of Lady Duff Gordon is also extremely interesting.   We can heartily recommend this work both for tone and workmanship."—*The Court Circular.*

"The pictures of female character to be found here are meet companions for young girls. . . . Much might be said both of the admirable choice of subject and of the picturesque and elevating method of treatment adopted. It need only be added that the volume is embellished by excellent portraits, and that it is issued in a very attractive manner."—*Nottingham Daily Guardian.*

"It is exactly a nice kind of book to give to a nice kind of girl; and, when you think of it, there are a lot of nice girls in this world of ours. They are good already—that of course—but a study of the lives of noble women will help them to be better; and goodness is of more consequence than anything else in the world."—*Glasgow Citizen.*

"Containing sketches of ten notable women of our time—the first Mary Somerville, the last Catherine Tait. It is the very book to give to a thoughtful girl."—*Glasgow Mail.*

"The history of several of the remarkable women who have adorned this century, is detailed, their gifts described, and their good deeds chronicled. For girls a more appropriate and inspiring book could not be placed in their hands."—*Edinburgh Daily Review.*

"Of special interest to South Londoners from the admirable biography it contains of the late Mrs. Tait, wife of the Archbishop of Canterbury."— *South London Press.*

"The sketches in every case give a comprehensive and interesting view of the life and labours of the persons dealt with."—*Aberdeen Free Press.*

"Of thoroughly sound and wholesome books for the season we have seen nothing better. The work is of great interest and value."—*Aberdeen Herald.*

"This book is far above the average of its class. It is so well-written that, once taken up, it is not easily laid down. The subjects selected are among the best, and they are representative in character. . . . There is an extremely fascinating account of Catherine Tait, wife of the Archbishop of Canterbury."—*Glasgow Herald.*

INDUSTRIAL CURIOSITIES: Glances here and there in the World of Labour.

Written and Edited by ALEXANDER HAY JAPP, LL.D.

F.R.S.L., F.R.S.E., F.R.G.S., F.S.A.

Double Crown, Extra 4s. 6d.

CONTENTS.

Leather.

Uses of Leather.

Wool.

Wool-Sorters' Disease.

Beds.

A Piece of Porcelain.

Needles.

The Sewing Machine.

At Chatham.

In a Hop Garden.

India Rubber.

Perfumes.

Gold and Silver.

Seals and Sealskins.

Photographs.

Clocks and Watches.

Locks and Safes.

The Post Office.

Through Traffic.

Appendix—

I. Postal Reforms.

II. Chromate Leather.

OPINIONS OF THE PRESS.

"Mr. Japp has found out quite a new field, and given a great deal of information which will prove new to most of his readers. Some of the subjects have been treated of before, yet even here Mr. Japp has managed to infuse much originality."— *Saturday Review.*

"An interesting volume, embracing a series of sketches, commencing with leather and ending with the post office. The author is well-known as a contributor to the magazines, and most of his "Glances" recently formed a feature in one of them, and they are worthy of republication."—*The Figaro.*

"Dr. A. H. Japp has collected into a handsome volume a series of papers which originally appeared in a condensed form in *Good Words* and other magazines, on a great variety of trades and manufactures. He begins with 'Leather' and ends with 'The Post Office.' Wherever he goes, whether among wool-sorters or needle makers, into a hop garden or a goldsmith's, with the photographer or the locksmith, he is quick to catch the salient features of the industry, and his descriptions are so lucid that we miss none of the points. Much of the information he has gleaned by personal inspection will be novel to the most of his readers; and the book is, on the whole, one of the most entertaining as well as instructive that can be imagined. The ladies will be sure to relish the chapters on the sewing-machine, needles, perfumes, seals and sealskins; and the book is one that will have a special charm for many classes of readers." —*North British Daily Mail.*

" A readable volume, describing the sights to be seen in many large factories; explaining the process of manufacture, and, by alluding to their progressive advances, relating their history, and in some instances, discussing the matters of science they involve. The information about ' Locks and Safes' is most instructive, many wonderful facts being stated."—*Dundee Advertiser.*

FOOTPRINTS: An Attempt to instil observation of Nature and the Love of It, by a familiar Record of Incidents connected with Men's relations to it in its many Phases.

By SARAH TYTLER,

Author of "The Huguenot Family," &c.

With many Illustrations.   Small Crown, 3s. 6d.

THE HOUSE BY THE WORKS:

By EDWARD GARRETT,

Author of " The Occupations of a Retired Life."

Cheap Edition, Crown 8vo., 5s.

OPINIONS OF THE PRESS.

" The girls with their Quaker and Moravian training, the worthy and benevolent Mrs. Pendlebury, and society generally, rich and poor, in Perford are depicted with skill."—*Daily News.*

"No writer succeeds better in bringing out the beauty of Puritanism—for even Puritanism has a beauty of its own, harsh and unlovely as in a general way it is apt to appear—than Mr. Edward Garrett, when, as in this story, he is altogether at his best. The picture he gives us here of the Enticknapp household, with its Moravian and Quaker traditions, is one nearly perfect of its kind for sobriety of taste and freedom from all sentimental exaggerations. In Lois Enticknapp, in particular, who is the real heroine of the tale, we have a very fine type of spiritual excellence, and she wins our sympathies so entirely that we are inclined to resent and protest against the cruel and all but crushing sorrow which the author is hardhearted enough to have in reserve for her. The story of Lydia Calderwood, again, is natural and very well managed ; nor can its theme, though an unpleasant one, be justly held out of place in a novel of the peculiar character of this."—*Graphic.*

"'The House by the Works' is, we think, the ripest of all the writings by the same hand, yielding itself less than some of the earlier ones to reflection, but presenting a masterly picture of life, relieved by lessons developed through fine character and fine influences dramatically justified and exhibited in action with the utmost faithfulness. What the author describes has been felt and known, not only in a general way, but down to circumstantials in some cases. We not only listen to a description of Perford with its industry and wealth, but are made to see it, and to see it with the help of an expert guide who can not only comment on the people, but unfold to us their inner motives. Lois Enticknapp and her mother—Lois, half-Quaker, half-Moravian, is one of the most original conceptions we remember, and Lydia Calderwood, an unfortunate, who, however, deserved to be fortunate, and struggled so nobly that the man who had wronged her at last returned to her to do right! The portraits of these three are very admirably done, and old Mrs. Enticknapp, the Quaker, with her aged and venerable assistants, carrying on her old-fashioned baker's business in that quiet and systematic way, is simply like a bit of delicious sketching from life. The rich household of the Prides, with its gaunt skeleton that cannot be confined to a cupboard, but will walk out and challenge sunlight and the gaze of the townspeople, in the form of a drunken mother, who in the end is revealed to us as no wife is, sad to say, only too like the style of things that goes on in large towns; but we are sorry for the rest of the Prides, and we do pity Kate Pride, with her true woman's heart, to the generous vein hid so sternly under hard cynicism and now and then affected recklessness."— *Nonconformist.*

"A thoughtfully-written, if not very exciting or absorbing story, and will be read with interest in these times of commercial crashes and trade depression. The materials out of which the novel has been woven are of the slightest. There is much sombreness in the tints, it is true, and Mr. Garrett unflinchingly draws the thin skin off the beauty of society, grapples the reader rigidly by the shoulder and sternly says to him, 'Look on that.' Yet there is tenderness in the same hand, practical generosity to the poor toilers, and sympathy with the suffering, as well as an under current of unbiassed religious feeling, which is as essential to the story as sunlight to the world."—*Dundee Advertiser, Jan.* 11, 1879.

POPULAR SCIENCE SERIES.

INSECT - LIFE : A Popular Introduction to Entomology, Profusely Illustrated.

Square Crown. Cloth extra, 3s. 6d.

PLANT-LIFE : Popular Papers on the Phenomena of Botany.

With 148 Illustrations drawn by the Author.

Square Crown. Cloth extra, 3s. 6d.

CONTENTS.

Microscopic Plants.
Plant Structure and Growth.
Fertilisation of Plants.
Predatory Plants.
Remarkable Leaves and Flowers.
About a Fern.
The Folk-lore of Plants.
Plants and Animals.
Mosses and Lichens.
Plants and Planets.
Horsetails and Stoneworts.
The Falling Leaf.
Fungi.
Algæ.

(Other volumes in preparation.)

THE HUMAN VOICE: A Practical Guide to

Public Speakers and Singers.

By Dr. J. Farrar, F.R.C.P.E.

With numerous Illustrations by the Author.

Small Crown, 3s. 6d.

EXTRACT FROM PREFACE.

" In introducing to the public this work, which was written several years ago, the Author may be allowed to say, that he was encouraged to persevere in the task by the feeling that he was labouring to supply a long-felt want,—a *popular* description, namely, of the organs and parts concerned in the production of the Faculty of Speech ; a description, that is, from which all unnecessary technicalities, and as much *dryness* as possible should be excluded, consistent with clearness and the acquisition of a general knowledge of the subject.

" There are, doubtless, thousands of readers, in-dependent of the strictly professional classes, to whom such knowledge—and especially the practical collateral information incidently treated of in the text—must prove of very great, if not of predomi-nant interest, and no small benefit. Indeed, the practical bearing and application of the facts educed have always been uppermost in the Author's mind, and have been throughout persistently inculcated.

"To public speakers, vocalists, &c., much pains have been taken to make the book a kind of Medical Guide or Companion—a sort of *vocal vade mecum*, to which reference may be made for information relating to the minor troubles, and some of the graver diseases, to which the vocal organs are liable, as well as the treatment of the more common ailments. This portion of the book will, it is believed, prove not the least acceptable and valuable of the whole."

Throughout the work will also be found a great number of useful hints and suggestions for the preservation of the vocal apparatus in health and efficiency. These, it is confidently anticipated, will very much enhance the interest and value of the book.

The illustrations, which have been inserted wherever found to be useful, will still further tend in this direction. The source of such of these as have been copied from other works are hereby thankfully acknowledged, and will be found enumerated in the list of illustrations.

THE WAY TO FORTUNE: A series of short

Essays, with Illustrative Proverbs and Anecdotes from

many sources.

Small Crown.   Cloth extra, 2s. 6d.

MASTER MISSIONARIES : Studies in Heroic
Pioneer Work.

By ALEXANDER H. JAPP, LL.D., F.R.S.E.
With Portraits and Illustrations.

Crown 8vo.   Cloth extra 4s. 6d.

CONTENTS.

OPINIONS OF THE PRESS.

"Recording the life-work of a number of men whom it is well to remember in these days of a good deal of 'inglorious ease.' Here we have many vivid pictures of dangers and difficulties which may be read with profit by all who are interested in missionary work, while they supply much information which will aid us to understand the history of our own times."—*Court Circular, Dec.* 11, 1880.

"A collection of sketches from the practised pen of Dr. Japp of men who have rendered good service to their race. All are graphic and very interesting."—*Nonconformist.*

"It brings before the reader a vivid conception of all the grandest chapters in pioneer effort throughout the world. There are many who must have felt the want of just such a handy book as this, and these will be grateful to Dr Japp."—*Glasgow Mail.*

"The new publishing firm has at once taken front rank in the character and style of the works it has brought before the public. This volume of biographies is a model. Dr. Japp is an accomplished *litterateur* who in the subjects he has here chosen has advantage of a hearty sympathy with their noble aims and aspirations. The art of abridgement is so skilfully practised that here we have no *hortus siccus*, but in every case a full length and life-like portrait of the subject. The leading incidents of each life are given with sufficient detail to show us the manner of man we are reading about."—*Edinburgh Christian Week.*

"The narratives contained in this volume are of great interest, and may be read by all with profit."—*Glasgow Herald.*

"They are printed in clear type and good paper, and are not too fine to be handled. To young people they teach the lesson how 'to make our lives sublime.'"—*Inverness Courier.*

"As a biographer, Dr. Japp occupies a high position. He is possessed of the art, and this combined with a pleasant style, makes all his works charming reading. In the present volume, the general reader will find much to interest and instruct, while those who feel an interest in the mission-field will find it of much service from the lessons that may be derived from the incidents related."—*Perthshire Advertiser.*

"We have seen no book of the kind to surpass this gracefully-written and nicely-illustrated volume."
—*Kilmarnock Standard.*

LEADERS OF MEN: a Book of Biographies
specially written for Young Men.
By H. A. Page, author of "Golden Lives."
Crown 8vo. Cloth extra, with portraits, 4s. 6d.

CONTENTS.

The Prince Consort.

Robert Dick, Baker and Geologist.

Commodore Goodenough.

George Moore.

John Duncan, Weaver and Botanist.

Samuel Greg.

Dr. John Wilson.

Dr. Andrew Reed.

Lord Lawrence.

OPINIONS OF THE PRESS.

"No one knows better than Mr. Page how to put within moderate compass the outstanding features of a life that has blessed the world so as to present a striking and impressive picture. This is just the volume to enlarge the views and to ennoble the aims of young men, and to such we specially commend it."—*Literary World.*

"Here is a book which should be in the hands of every boy in the Kingdom in whose mind it is desirable to implant a true ideal of life, and a just notion of the proper objects of ambition ; and we may congratulate Mr. Page upon having carried out his task with all possible care and skill. 'Leaders of Men' is every way an admirable volume."— *Court Circular.*

"Well and tersely written, and will no doubt find a public."—*Manchester Guardian.*

"Although we do not as a rule regard the republication of such sketches with approval, Mr. Page has done his work so well that we make an exception of this volume."—*Figaro.*

"A volume of carefully-prepared sketches, including a memoir of the late Prince Consort, showing how he strove to fulfil his idea of duty as the 'husband of the Queen, the tutor of the royal children, the private secretary to the Sovereign, and her permanent minister;' Sketches of Robert Dick of Thurso, 'a man who found a true satisfaction in his daily work, although nothing less practical than that of a baker, but who yet made noble contributions to geological science;' of George Moore; of Commodore Goodenough, and others, not forgetting Lord Lawrence who rendered invaluble services to his country in our Indian possessions."—*Nonconformist.*

"Readable examples . . . . . with original comment and reflection judiciously intermixed."—*Scotsman.*

"These biographies can only be spoken of in terms of cordial praise. The facts are evidently drawn from the best sources; they are narrated in an exceedingly attractive style: and each memoir contains information which not only the young, but many readers of mature age will be glad to avail themselves of."—*Nottingham Guardian.*

"Instructive and tastefully-written biographies.

For boys in particular the work is an admirable one."—*Aberdeen Herald.*

"Of the many publications for youth at the Christmas season, we are sure that 'Leaders of Men' will command a high place in the estimation of boys. In it we have short biographical notices, not only of men born to command, but also of those who, by industry and perseverance, raised themselves from the working-classes to high positions in the scientific and commercial world. The book opens with a graphic sketch of the late Prince Consort. The volume is replete with matter of the most attractive description, and cannot fail to rivet the attention not only of young readers, but also of those of riper years,"—*Edinburgh Daily Review.*

"It is a capital book for boys, full of high teaching and noble incentive. Happy are the boys and girls of this generation, who have such writers to cater for them."—*Glasgow Citizen.*

"Will prove very acceptable to a great many people who have not time to read big books. . . The memoirs are written in a clear and animated style, and embrace the essential facts in the detailed biography of each person."—*Inverness Courier.*

"Excellent examples of a kind of writing in which boys take great delight, and as such may be honestly recommended to other circles of readers."—*Glasgow Herald.*

"Instructive and tastefully written biographies. For boys in particular, the work is a most admirable one, though it may be read with profit and pleasure by many others."—*Aberdeen Daily Free Press.*

GERMAN LIFE AND LITERATURE :
In a series of Biographical Studies.

By ALEXANDER H. JAPP, LL.D. 8vo., 12s.

CONTENTS.

Lessing.
Winckelmann.
Moses Mendelssohn
Herder.
Goethe.
Ludwig Tieck.
Novalis.
Romantic Element in German Literature.
German Philosophy and Political Life.

OPINIONS OF THE PRESS.

" Dr. Japp writes with profound and varied knowledge, and the thoroughness and earnestness with which in nearly every instance he has done his work deserve hearty recognition. He calls no man master in the sense that he has accepted, no readings of character, and no interpretation of works at second hand. His judgments of Lessing, Herder, and Goethe in particular, are marked by independence and individuality. Those who have made special studies of these great writers will be the first to acknowledge a debt to Dr. Japp, when they have read his estimates and remarks. His criticism of the strong points of Lessing, for example, is acute and often subtle, yet he never loses sight in the multitude of details of the main object in which he is intent, of drawing the man and his work, showing in his character and career, and what has been done and achieved through these, in relation to German literature. There is much refinement of analysis in the study of Herder, which places that comprehensive genius on the high pedestal, from which he commands the admiration and yet attracts the sympathy of thinkers, for Herder was a writer for thinkers rather than for the mass.   More elaborate than either of these, and not less thorough and careful is the study of Goethe. . . . We do not agree with all the judgments we find here on the individual work of the great German, but we welcome with sincere satisfaction an effective and serious protest against that tyranny of art for art's sake, which has come to be common in England and Germany, to the detriment often of honour, morality, and simple faith."—*The Globe.*

"On one point we cannot but think that the view here given of Lessing is more correct than that generally received.   Dr. Japp has shown conclusively that Lessing was not a mere rude denier of inspiration and revelation, but a profound believer in certain fundamental truths. . . . Those who wish to know Lessing as a theologian, and who cannot read the language in which he wrote, will find a sufficiently full account of his opinions in this volume.   It is with regret that we leave unquoted many passages of beauty bearing upon religion, as apprehended by Lessing and Mendelssohn. . . . This book is not one that can be borrowed from a circulating library, and read profitably through in a few days.   It is one to which the student of letters will often recur.   We cordially recommend it to our readers."—*Nonconformist.*

"Dr. Japp has treated his subject exhaustively and from many points of view.   But perhaps none of these essays will be read at this time with a livelier interest than that on Moses Mendelssohn.

His story is a noble and inspiring one, and here it is worthily told. . . . These observations can only serve to indicate very feebly the scope of Dr. Japp's really great work. It deals throughout in a solid manner with its subject, and does so in a style which is singularly lucid and free from the oracular obscurity which seems to be so attractive to most writers on German literature. It is an admirable book, by an able writer."—*The Court Circular*.

"It contains most interesting reading, some admirable bits of biography, and also some incisive and original criticism."—*Glasgow Citizen*.

"This is a book that is worthy of a more extended notice than we can give. Dr. Japp has succeeded in gleaning not a few facts of the greatest importance hitherto overlooked, while in the case of others, such as Mendelssohn and Winckelmann, he has been able to give for the first time to English readers an adequate idea of their life and influence. The book is scholarly and masterly, and will be none the less welcome that, in some points, notably with regard to Goethe, the author runs counter to generally accepted opinions and estimates."—*The Christian World*.

"A very interesting volume. We trust that Dr. Japp's labours will meet with the reward they deserve, and that the demand for this book may be such as to induce him at some future time to give us a second series of his studies."—*Trübner's Oriental and Foreign Record*.

"A critical, deep, and refined analysis of a portion of German literature. In a series of articles, Dr. Japp gives a number of biographies of Lessing,

Winckelmann, Mendelssohn, and others, and a keenly critical estimate of their work. He sharply discriminates their merits and faults, and determines with much solid argument their relative positions. Students of the great German dramatists will read his biting criticisms with interest."—*Dundee Advertiser.*

"We lay aside Dr. Japp's volume with the feeling that is the fruit of careful and loving study, and that in it we have the most valuable contibution of recent years to the history of German literature."— *Glasgow Herald.*

"Gives, as no previous work known to us gives, a wonderfully lucid and concise conception of the course of German thought and culture, and of the leading forces which have partly moulded, partly been moulded by it, since that great Aufklärung, which ushered in Germany's splendid and first truly national literary epoch. When to this we add that, throughout his present volume, Dr. Japp writes with all his accustomed ease and flow of style, it will be seen that he has produced for us a work which has the merit of being extremely readable as well as interesting and instructive. . . . The study of Lessing, with which he starts in his survey, is admirable and sympathetic, recognising in Lessing, as he does, the forerunner and prime mover of the whole subsequent intellectual upheaval. . . The analysis of Lessing's life and work is as admirable for clearness and conciseness of treatment as it is for the many points of fresh interest revealed in them. It need hardly be said that the effect of both is to deepen our impression of the beauty and nobleness of Lessing's character, and to make us feel how important and enduring has been his influence."—*Aberdeen Daily Free Press.*

THE TREASURE BOOK OF CONSOLA-
TION : for all in Sorrow or Suffering.

Compiled and Edited by Benjamin Orme, M.A.,
Editor of "The Treasure Book of Devotional Reading."

Crown 8vo. Cloth extra. 3s. 6d.

OPINIONS OF THE PRESS.

" The book is a striking testimony to the fact
that, whatever else Christianity may be, it is em-
phatically a power that consoles. Pain and sorrow,
as mirrored in these extracts, are no accidents of
human life, not evil to be endured with what firm-
ness a man may, but something by which life is
made wider, deeper, purer, and infinitely more
glorious than it otherwise could have been. Pain
is transfigured in the light of a larger life, when it is
accepted by the sufferer as a step towards the grand
optimism of Christianity, in which all things are regarded as working together for good. With great
taste and judgment, and with wide Catholicity of
sentiment, Mr. Orme has made his selections. His
book is, indeed, a book of consolation. We believe
it will find a welcome in many a household, and
help many who suffer to bear their pain hopefully."
—*Spectator.*

" The Editor has ably performed his labour of
love, and has, in this volume, opened a fountain of
thought from which refreshing streams should go
forth to console, to strengthen, and to nerve for
fresh effort many grief-stricken mourners."—*Nonconformist.*

" The book is well arranged ; we have sections
or chapters which treat of sorrow or grief generally,
on fortune and the loss of fortune, on the loss of
friends, the loss of children, on sickness and pain,
old age, and on sorrow for sin. Then come sections
dealing with the sources of consolation. . . .
Mr. Orme has certainly been industrious, as the
reader will gather from the fact that nearly two
hundred different authors are laid under contri-
bution for this book, not counting anonymous
writers and extracts from magazines. ' The Treasure Book of Consolation' is admirably selected
and edited in every respect, and should be welcome
in every household in the land."—*Court Circular.*

" We cannot remember a book of this class which
covers the whole subject so well as the volume
before us. The selections are judiciously and aptly
chosen, traverse the whole field of English literature,
and are dexterously dovetailed into each other.
The book is sumptuously printed and handsomely
got up."—*Literary World.*

" To all who are in sorrow or suffering we may
safely commend this ' Treasure-Book.' . . . .
Mr. Orme has made the selection in a truly Catholic
spirit, with exquisite taste, and also with a delicate
spiritual discernment and a keen insight into human
needs. His book will be the means of carrying
comfort to many a troubled heart."—*The Freeman.*
" The excerpts are vey appropriate and well-
classified. . . . There is much to admire in
this volume, much that is very touching."—*Literary
Churchman.*

"We most heartily commend Mr. Orme's Treasure-Book,' which exhibits industrious, untiring
research and careful editing, and which is, moreover,
very beautifully printed and bound."—*The Teacher.*

"The richest variety of consolatory words from
the best authors. The tasteful style in which the
volume has been got up corresponds with its
literary and spiritual value. A more fitting present
for a friend in sorrow or suffering it would be hard
to find."—*Glasgow Mail.*

"This is a book for all at some stage of their
lives, and for many at more than one stage. . . .
The extracts have been made over a wide range,
and very judiciously ; and the book is most tastefully got up."—*Aberdeen Daily Free Press.*

LITERARY BYE-HOURS: A Book of Instructive
Pastime.

By H. A. PAGE.

Square Small Crown.   2s. 6d.

Containing *Vers de Société* and Parody, with typical
Illustrations of all present-day styles.

EXTRACT FROM PREFACE.

"To mingle the instructive and the amusing, in
fit and fair proportion, is no easy task, but this is
what the author of the present little volume has
aimed at. Goethe, not without a certain uncon-
scious self-revelation, said sneeringly of parody: "I
have never concealed what an implacable enemy I
am to all parody and travesty ; but it is only on

this account that I am so, because this base brood pulls down the noble, the beautiful, the great in order to make an end of them." Notwithstanding the sneer of so great a master, the author believes that, when viewed in a proper spirit, parody may be both instructive and amusing. When some part of the portion here given on that subject appeared in the *British Quarterly Review*, it was received with peculiar favour ; the *Spectator* remarking : " There is some admirable criticism in ' Parody and Parodists.' We have never seen the real nature of parody better defined." The author trusts that none of his kindly critics may have any reason now to change their opinion of the essays of which they before spoke so favourably."

HANDBOOKS FOR THE HOME.

EASY LESSONS IN BOTANY. By the Author of "Plant-Life."

Also adapted for the use of schools, according to the requirements of the Education Department as published in the Revised Code, Fourth Schedule.

Small Double Crown. Stiff Covers. 6d.

THE AQUARIUM : How to begin and how to maintain it.

SUNDAY DUTY : A manual to aid in a profitable and pleasant use of the day.

THRIFT.

FERNS AND FERNERIES. By the Author of
"How to Detect the Adulterations of Food."

"In this work it has been our intention as far as possible to guide our readers to the grateful end, when after days of toil they see around them proofs of their studied labour. Like nearly all work which springs from a healthy brain, the cultivation of Ferns gives its own reward. To an inventive mind the following work is but a suggestion, and to him the expense will be but nominal. The Author would be pleased to receive any suggestions in regard to future editions, as he desires to make the work useful to the million."

OPINIONS OF THE PRESS.

"This is a useful little *brochure* of about fifty pages, on the cultivation of a fernery. The first twenty-two pages are devoted to the description of a selection from our British ferns adapted for culture, with details of their fructification and germination. A selection of wild flowers suitable for growth conjointly with ferns is a good idea. Then follow directions for securing suitable soils, &c., while the pamphlet ends with a synopsis of the chief group of British ferns."—*Academy.*

"We cordially recommend it as the best little *brochure* on Ferns we have yet seen. Its merits far exceed those of much larger and more pretentious works."—*Science Gossip.*

"In brief compass, and without wasting words, it tells all that is necessary to be known for the general cultivation of these lovely plants."—*Literary World.*

"To the cultivator of this pleasing study this little book will be found of great utility. We heartily commend the work to those in search of a new pleasure."—*Perthshire Advertiser and Citizen.*

"Anyone who is desirous to cultivate ferns cannot do better than procure this nicely-illustrated little book."—*Greenock Telegraph.*

"This little book will doubtless meet with a hearty reception. It is written in a plain and concise style, and the subject is dealt with practically and, at the same time, attractively. A large amount of information is thus contained in a few well-printed pages, which are illustrated by a number of clever drawings by the author."—*Maidstone Standard.*

"Full of charming illustrations, exact scientific information, and practical guidance."—*Glasgow Mail.*

"Anyone who is ambitious of knowing all about ferns, and how to cultivate them, cannot do better than procure this charming little work."—*Kilmarnock Standard.*

HEALTH-AT-HOME SERIES. By popular Authors.

Small Crown. Stiff Covers. 9d.

Air and Ventilation.

How we Live and Grow; the principles of Physiology simply Illustrated.

How to Detect the Adulterations of Food.

Dress.

Health and Work.

The House and Furnishing.

Food and Cooking.

THE BATH AND BATHING. By Dr. J. FARRAR, F.R.C.P.E.

OPINION OF THE PRESS.

"Not the least interesting portion of 'The Bath and Bathing' is the historical sketch which occupies the opening chapter. We are astonished to-day at the rapid growth of hydropathic establishments in Great Britain, and especially in Scotland ; but what are they all compared with the baths that were built in Rome by Caracalla nearly seventeen centuries ago ! . . . This book only costs ninepence ; but it really contains all that is essential in the way of warning and suggestions to bathers, whether at the seaside, in the inland river, at the public baths, or in their own private houses.—*North British Mail.*

(Others of the Series in preparation).

HEROIC ADVENTURE : Narratives of recent endurance and suffering in the process of Discovery.

From Livingstone and Burton to Schweinfurth and Nordenskjöld.

With Illustrations and Portraits.

Small Crown. Cloth extra 3s. 6d.

ENGLISH POEMS IN GERMAN DRESS :
An easy and pleasant aid to acquiring the German Language. Square Crown, 3s. 6d.

AN ENGLISH GRAMMAR FOR SCHOOLS.
Adapted to the Requirements of the Revised Code. In Two Parts. Price 3½d. each. Or both in one cover, 6d.

A POETICAL READER FOR SCHOOLS,
arranged on an entirely new principle, with Illustrations specially done for the work. In two parts.

VIVISECTION, scientifically and ethically considered, in Prize Essays. By JAMES MACAULAY, A.M., M.D., F.R.S.E. ; the Rev. BREWIN GRANT, B.A., Vicar of St. Paul's, Bethnal Green, London, E.; and ABIATHUR WALL, L.R.C.P.E., Member of the Royal College, England, &c.

THE ONE SHILLING SERIES OF PRIZE BOOKS, which will include Stories by the best Authors, well Illustrated. Mr. H. A. PAGE and Miss SARAH TYTLER will be among the writers.

THE EIGHTEENPENNY SERIES OF STORY BOOKS, which will contain first-class tales, admirably Illustrated

I. The "Starry Blossom," and and other Stories. By M. Betham Edwards, Author of "Minna's Birthday," &c.
Illustrations by Miss Joanna Samworth.

II. "Dan Stapleton's Last Ride." By the Author of "Morag," &c.

III. "Sister Edith's Probation." By E. Conder Gray.

IV. "The Three Beauties" and the "Three Frights." By Sarah Tytler.

A NORTH COUNTRY PASTORAL, and other Stories.
By the Author of "Cleveden." In three volumes.

HALF-HOLIDAY HANDBOOKS: Guides to Rambles Round London. With Maps and Illustrations. Crown 8vo. 9d. each.

I. **KINGSTON-ON-THAMES & DISTRICT.**
—Ham Common.—The King's Stone.—Mill Lane.—Kingston Common.—Ditton Hill.—Long Ditton.—Claygate Lane.—Ditton Wood.—Claygate Common. — Chessington Wood. — Esher Common.— Stoke Wood.—Ashley Park.—Weybridge Common. —St. George's Hill, &c.

II. **ROUND REIGATE** : by a Resident. The Town.— The Park.—The Hill.— Gatton.— Earlswood—Nutfield.—Redhill—The Reformatory Farm-School.—Buckland. — Betchworth. — Box Hill. — Leigh.—Merstham.—Bletchingly, etc.

III. **DORKING & DISTRICT**: The Town Betchworth Park.—Box Hill and Mickleham.—Ranmer. — Deepdene. — Westcott. — Wotton. — Abinger.— Redlands Wood.— The Holmwood.—Coldharbour.—Leith Hill.—Broom Hall.—Tanhurst. —Ockley, &c.

IV. **ROUND RICHMOND.**—The Town, Past and Present.—The Palace.—Kew and the Gardens. —The Hill and the Park.—By the Thames.—Richmond to Barnes.—Petersham.—Ham.— Kingston —Twickenham.—Strawberry Hill.—Teddington.— Isleworth. — Brentford. — Wimbledon. — Sheen.— Mortlake.

V. Round Maidstone.

VI. Round Sydenham.

VII. Greenwich and District.

VIII. From Croydon to Leatherhead.

IX. Round Tunbridge Wells.

X. Round Bromley.

XI. Guide to Geology of the London Basin.

Bowers Bros., Steam Printers, London, S.E.